Why?

BECAUSE WE STILL LIKE YOU

Why?

BECAUSE WE STILL LIKE YOU

AN ORAL HISTORY OF THE *Mickey Mouse Club*®

JENNIFER ARMSTRONG

GC

GRAND CENTRAL
PUBLISHING

NEW YORK   BOSTON

Grand Central Publishing
Hachette Book Group
237 Park Avenue
New York, NY 10017

www.HachetteBookGroup.com

Printed in the United States of America

First Edition: October 2010

10 9 8 7 6 5 4 3 2 1

Grand Central Publishing is a division of Hachette Book Group, Inc.
The Grand Central Publishing name and logo is a trademark of Hachette
Book Group, Inc.

Library of Congress Cataloging-in-Publication Data
Armstrong, Jennifer.
Why? because we still like you : an oral history of the Mickey Mouse Club /
Jennifer Armstrong.—1st ed.
      p. cm.
Summary: "An oral history of the Mickey Mouse Club show,
featuring interviews with Mouseketeers and people involved with
the show, along with commentary about how it became a
pop culture phenomenon."—Provided by the publisher.
Includes bibliographical references and index.
ISBN 978-0-446-54595-2
1. Mickey Mouse Club (Television program)   I. Title.
PN1992.77.M53A76 2010
791.45'75—dc22
2010013876

To my family—Dad, Mom, Scott, and Julie—
for always making me feel like a child star

Contents

Contents

Acknowledgments

Journalism is difficult without willing subjects, and this book would've been impossible without the witty, articulate, helpful showbiz pros known as the former Mouseketeers being willing to share their precious life stories with me. They became my teen idols fifty-plus years after the fact. Mr. Disney would, indeed, be proud. This book, however, simply would not exist if not for my tireless editor, Celia Johnson, who also patiently walked me through my first book. Agent Nicole Steen played matchmaker and changed my life in the process.

Emily Winter took on the arduous task of transcribing my early interviews, and Joe Lynch did the same with reams and reams of my later interviews. This book could not have happened in any reasonable amount of time without them and their fearless Google-researching abilities. My esteemed *Entertainment Weekly* colleague Ken Tucker—a true role model—shared his childhood love for *The Mickey Mouse Club* with me in both early and late stages of this book, which informed my approach immensely. Former Disney

Acknowledgments

librarian Paula Sigman-Lowery was generous with her endless knowledge of the subject and her affection for the show. Allison Hantschel and Tanner Stransky provided emotional support early and often; Heather Wood Rudulph kept our business going and, with her husband Ken, provided my second home in Los Angeles; and Dave Freiberg gave me shelter in Sacramento and continuous encouragement. Paul Katz provided all of the following: encyclopedic TV knowledge, emotional support, a lightning-fast read of a much longer first draft, more emotional support, a hell of a lot of wine, and even, for better or worse, Mouse ears. I shudder to think how long it would take me to repay such favors, but luckily, we're not keeping score (right?). And Jesse Davis didn't just take a great author photo (if I do say so myself)—he also kept me going during some critical stages of this book. I didn't know how much I needed him until he showed up.

I must also thank *Entertainment Weekly* overall for nine destiny-altering years of top-notch training in professional pop culture punditry and the most supportive editor a girl could have, Henry Goldblatt, for helping me carve out the time for this project. Long live smart, classy entertainment journalism.

Author's Note

This book is based on interviews with several of the original Mouseketeers as well as published accounts of their time on *The Mickey Mouse Club*. Unfortunately, some of the major figures involved in the show's success—including Walt Disney, adult "Mooseketeers" Jimmie Dodd and Roy Williams, and Mouseketeer Cheryl Holdridge—have died. Standout Mouseketeer Darlene Gillespie was unreachable for comment after years of being out of touch with her former costars. And the most well-known Mouseketeer of all, Annette Funicello, can no longer participate in interviews due to her now twenty-year-plus battle with multiple sclerosis. Where possible, these key players' perspectives are represented by their previous interviews and writings about their Mouseketeer experiences.

Part 1

MAKING A PHENOMENON

Chapter One

Introduction

Lonnie Burr's blond hair would be just so: the sides slicked back, the top a forever-cresting wave rising above his smooth forehead and breaking along the back of his skull. And then, as usual, one of the paunchy *Mickey Mouse Club* producers would come along and flatten the twelve-year-old Mouseketeer's coif with one glunk of his black-winged beanie straight onto the top of his head, suctioning it to his cranium and cutting a line across his eyebrows as if, perhaps, his brain might come off with it if squeezed tightly enough. A guy could have the coolest hair in town, but no one would know about it if he wore his Mouseketeer cap according to regulation. This fact alone made many of the older, teenage boys among *The Mickey Mouse Club*'s two dozen cast members hate those ears that would become such icons of the 1950s. Pompadours were the rage. The guys had to have their waves out. And producers' demands that they wear the stupid hats way down on their heads wrecked everything. "All the guys hated the ears," Lonnie says now. "They'd always want us to wear it like a monk."

The solution: the boys would act like they were going along with the producers' ridiculous rules until the last second before shooting started, then sneak the cap back two inches or so, just as cameras started to roll, pushing as much hair as possible forward with it to approximate a decent wave. After all, they'd spent most of their preparation time in the morning washing, drying, parting, combing, dovetailing, and applying a gooey wave-set product that would dry as hard as glue, just to do it all over again and again throughout the day as they sweated through their dance numbers. It was the dawn of the rock 'n' roll era, and hair was a priority. So time and again, Lonnie and castmates Bobby Burgess and Tommy Cole would be there on the Mouseketeer soundstage, fidgeting a fraction of a second before the scene, doffing their caps to liberate their waves just as cameras started to roll. "If you watch the show, you can see the different sizes of waves out front," Lonnie says. "All of us boys had full manes of hair, and they wanted none of it showing," Tommy says. "The girls all still looked pretty because they had these waves of hair flowing down, but they wanted to make the boys look like little bald people!"

Yet when the stage bells rang to signal the cameras were rolling and the director called for "action!" you'd never know the angst those ears were causing the boys. The faces beneath the hats would smile like that day was the best one of their young lives as they tapped, twirled, and sang their way through songs about everything from the importance of drinking milk to bicycle safety to cooking with Minnie Mouse. The millions of kids watching from home on the other side of the screen soaked it all in, oblivious to even the slightest hint that their favorite TV stars could be anything except cheerful. After all, the cast of Mouseketeers—known as "Mice" to those on the inside—were the most popular kids in the country, the envy of every kid growing up in the mid-1950s, privileged members of the fairy-tale-perfect Walt Disney family.

At five p.m. every weekday, just when homework had started to feel unbearable but dinner was still simmering on the stove, youthful fans would rush to the television sets their parents had just purchased, click the dial to ABC, and sing along from the opening "Mickey Mouse Club March" to the final "Alma Mater" sign-off. They'd delight in the four fifteen-minute segments of the daily show: the newsreel, the Mouseketeers' performance (which could include skits, dance numbers, circus acts, or performing guests, depending on the day), the Mickey Mouse cartoon, and the unfolding drama of serials such as *The Adventures of Spin and Marty* and *The Hardy Boys*. Though the Mouseketeers were only a portion of the show, they were the part the fans cared about: Loyal viewers wanted to belong to any club that included these kids who seemed to know how to do anything and everything.

After *The Mickey Mouse Club* premiered on October 3, 1955, the kiddie shows airing in its time slot on the other networks moved out of its way, and for good reason: Walt Disney was a force to be reckoned with when it came to programming to families at that time, and the master had outdone himself once again. *The Mickey Mouse Club* brought glitzy production values and true entertainment to its child audiences, which it took seriously. The Mouseketeers may have accounted for only a quarter of the hourlong broadcast, but the real secret ingredient was the youthful cast. Raved *Los Angeles Times* critic Walter Ames the day of the show's debut, "Any one of these children could be a star in his or her own right."

More than ten million children watched the first season of *The Mickey Mouse Club,* and two million Mouse ears sold in the show's first three months, proving that kids mattered in this new mass-communication-driven world. *The Mickey Mouse Club* demonstrated that a group of ordinary children could put on a crowd-pleasing show and that kids their age would tune in en masse to watch it. The series spoke straight to the prepubescent crowd at a pivotal time in their lives, when they were primed to fixate on anything they felt was just for them. *The Mickey Mouse Club* made a generation of kids feel like they belonged to their own elite group, a feeling that would lodge itself in their hearts and make them remember Mouseketeers Annette, Tommy, Darlene, Cubby, Karen, Lonnie, Sherry, Doreen, and the rest of the gang for the rest of their lives.

The kids glued to their TV sets every evening for *The Mickey Mouse Club* could rattle off the five theme days easier than they could recite the Pledge of Allegiance: Monday's Fun with Music, Tuesday's Guest Star Day, Wednesday's Anything Can Happen, Thursday's Circus Day, Friday's Talent Round-Up. They knew the nine most popular Mouseketeers by name as they sounded off in Roll Call: Annette! Tommy! Darlene! Bobby! Doreen! Cubby!

Karen! Lonnie! Sharon! And having a favorite Mouseketeer was as important as having a best friend. A four-year-old girl watching in California might idolize Doreen for her wide-eyed beauty. A twelve-year-old boy in Illinois might covet famed Mouseketeer sweetheart Annette Funicello so much that he'd spend most of his viewing time grumbling with jealousy that guys like Lonnie and Bobby got to be so near the dark-haired goddess. A five-year-old boy in Maryland might see host Jimmie Dodd playing the guitar and make one of his own out of a cardboard box and rubber bands. Moms would encourage it all, happy to have the kids settled down for an hour and even happier that they were watching those pleasant Mouseketeers sing such nice songs.

With *The Mickey Mouse Club*, kids could be part of the action. Fans could sign up to be official members of the Club, call themselves Mouseketeers in good standing—and even show proof if they sent in for a membership card. Belonging felt as essential as joining the Boy or Girl Scouts, complete with hats and theme songs. Viewers might even get a shot at appearing on Talent Round-Up Day—which featured "real" kids playing the trumpet, twirling the baton, performing magic, or any number of special skills—at mass auditions held at department stores throughout the country. They could play Club records, carry a Club lunchbox, strum a toy Club guitar. In short, *The Mickey Mouse Club* would extend into kids' everyday lives far beyond its five p.m. time slot.

The Mickey Mouse Club audience may have felt included in the larger sense of Club membership, but viewers still wished more than anything that they could be among the real, televised Mouseke-teers—even future blockbuster auteur John Hughes. The director spent his formative years watching *The Mickey Mouse Club*, and the envy he felt for its stars became a major force behind his drive for success. "I used to watch *The Mickey Mouse Club*, those obnox-ious, spoiled Mouseketeers you just wanted to beat the tar out of," groused the man behind box-office megahits such as *National Lam-poon's Vacation*, *Sixteen Candles*, and *Home Alone* in a 1994 inter-view. "They could do anything! Disneyland after hours? Whatever you want! They'd wear these horse things, and they'd give away giant Tootsie Rolls. My grandmother was diabetic; there was a fear of sugar in my house. I wanted one of those goddamn Tootsie Rolls, I wanted to dance with that horse for a while, I wanted to go to Disneyland. I never got there as a kid and knew I never would."

However maddening it felt, back in the '50s, every kid wanted to be a Mouseketeer. This book tells the behind-the-scenes story of what that was like—how *The Mickey Mouse Club* changed both the worlds of those kids beneath the iconic caps and the entertain-ment landscape at large. It explores how the series paved the way for all that came after—from its humble beginnings as a marketing ploy for Disneyland through its short but mesmerizing run to the numerous resurrections that cemented its place in the hearts of sev-eral generations—all through the recollections of those who made it a phenomenon. It reveals how a group of regular kids—from the Los Angeles suburbs and the projects, from plugged-in Hollywood families and working-class immigrant parents—lived often-regular lives despite the hot glare of the spotlight. First crushes, cool-kid cliques, heartbreaking rejections, and homecoming queens—or at least a girl named Annette Funicello who looked just like one—were as much a part of their lives as promotional tours, Disneyland appearances, dance routines, lights, cameras, and action.

Their story involves too-tight sweaters, multimillion-dollar corporate risks, and spin the bottle. Along the way, idols were born, dreams were crushed, and a heck of a lot of felt beanies with plastic ears on them were sold. This book was written without authorization from the Walt Disney Company, so it presents as balanced a picture of Mousekelife as possible, from the Mice who embrace their childhood fame to those who wish they'd never called themselves Mice. It will tell of where they all ended up, even if they hardly lived Disney fairy tales: Some landed on the squeaky-clean variety program *The Lawrence Welk Show*, others in nude photo layouts; some starred in beach movies, others came out of the closet in *Rolling Stone*; some went to therapy, others went to jail.

In certain parts of the story, legend has likely overtaken memory. All we can do now is tell things the way the Mice who can still share their recollections recount them more than fifty years later, even if those memories have been marred or reshaped by time. Who knows? Perhaps the myths—the way the raw material of reality has settled into the grooves of the Mouseketeer legacy—have their own unique value.

In any case, their legend began in dance classes across Southern California, where future Mice were tapping their way through after-school instruction—some put there by stage parents hoping it would lead to a big break, others by harried parents looking for their own break from their hyperactive youngsters. It began at kiddie ballets and band performances, amateur contests and accordion recitals—events that would only be the beginning of something much bigger. To make this new kind of television show, the kind filled with young stars every kid in America would want to be, casting would be key. And Walt Disney was about to bring his magic touch to the lives of more than two dozen unsuspecting little unknowns.

Chapter Two

From Dance Class to the Disney Lot

Doreen Tracey sat behind the desk at the Rainbow Studio, her huge green eyes blank with boredom, a state the little firebrand didn't tolerate well. She'd just turned twelve, old enough now to help out at her parents' dance-class business, but manning the phone while her dad was next door playing cards with buddies wasn't her idea of thrilling. Then came the call that changed that. The one from a man named Jack Lanvin. "I'm a casting director at Disney Studios," he announced. "I'd like to get some of your best kids from the school there out to audition for a new show."

All of a sudden a mischievous smile and sparkling eyes were competing for attention on her moon-shaped countenance. Her killer showbiz instinct—passed down from Mom and Dad, the onetime international dance team Tracey and Hay—kicked in. Without a doubt *she* could call herself one of the best dancers at the studio. Maybe not *the* best, but... "Oh, I know a little girl who would be just *perfect* for your auditions," she told him.

Her father agreed to take her to try out, despite his reservations about allowing his daughter to get mixed up in a long-term show-business job beyond the fleeting roles she'd already done against his better judgment (one uncredited part in 1953's Betty Grable musical *The Farmer Takes a Wife* and an appearance on *The Colgate Comedy Hour*). Those were the sorts of accidental detours into Hollywood life that have always been known to just happen to kids growing up in Los Angeles. But now that she wanted to try out for a Walt Disney venture, he couldn't much argue against his daughter's audition ambitions. "My father didn't want me to audition, but it seemed a little schizophrenic of him to say when you're in the business of a dance studio where the best in the business come to rehearse," Doreen says now. "So he let me."

Doreen wanted to keep the audition a secret from the rest of the studio, but that her father wouldn't allow. To her chagrin, he posted the information for all of his students to see. She wondered if her meager professional experience was enough. Like any kid trying out for a team she *desperately* wanted to make, she didn't want to invite still more competition.

Soon, however, she had far more competition to worry about than a couple dozen kids from her dad's dance studio, as she learned when she found herself crammed into the Disney Studios commissary with hundreds of other hopefuls on a muggy spring day in 1955, breathing in rank kid sweat. Dressed in a Little Bo Peep–style hoop skirt, all frilly innocence, she was preparing to tear into a plaintive ballad by Patti Page. (What she didn't have in glitzy credits she made up for with an ironic sense of humor.) She eyed her rivals as they milled about her, practicing their steps and warming up their voices for their parents and dance teachers. There was a cluster of kids from retired ballerina Burch Mann's studio up in Alhambra, just north of Los Angeles; a tiny boy named Cubby O'Brien who could flip his sticks while playing some serious drum solos; and a sleepy-eyed teenage guy named Tommy Cole dressed in full mariachi gear and lugging an accordion; among others.

Much of what Doreen saw around the waiting area intimidated her, a rare feeling for the born performer. She felt at home around Hollywood; her parents were showbiz vets who had worked up a vaudeville act together and had since retired from dancing to open a club called Slappy Maxie's on Wilshire Boulevard as well as the Rainbow Studio, where kids took tap, ballet, and jazz alongside celebrities such as Debbie Reynolds. Doreen usually had so much natural confidence that she was often picked to be the center of attention in any given group number at the studio, to ham it up, deliver the joke, play the lead, serve as the ringmaster in the circus. (She had even literally served as the ringmaster in an all-girls circus once.) But now she couldn't stop thinking, *I'm not as good a tap dancer as these guys. I'm in trouble.*

When her time came to face *The Mickey Mouse Club*'s producers, she put her worries about the other kids out of her head, took a deep breath, and focused on her audition act, which she'd come up with herself. She knew it was good—it had killed when she performed it during a Rainbow Studio recital. She may not have danced or sung *better than everyone else*, but she was good at both;

and the one thing she did have over others was personality. She reminded herself she also had a father who owned a dance studio that could help the Disney people recruit more talent. That had to count for something. In her pantaloons and skirt, she put on her serious face and ripped into Page's account of a wayward soul. By the time she got to the chorus, the producers' smiles were turning into admiring chuckles. "It was quite funny, and it got a lot of laughs," she recalls. "The minute I saw their expressions, I knew I got the job. You can just tell, you know?"

Doreen would be one of twenty-eight kids in whom Disney executives would spot a glint of star potential in the course of auditioning hundreds of kids culled from local dance classes, recitals, and the like. Amateur contest veteran Bobby Burgess would drive up from Long Beach, an hour south of Los Angeles, looking to break into acting in a serial called *Spin and Marty*. Singer Tommy Cole would hope his voice outweighed his lack of dancing skills. Sharon Baird and Lonnie Burr would come with résumés already weighty with experience, while Karen Pendleton would show up having never even been on a Hollywood set. All of them would find a place in the sprawling cast of Disney's chancy new TV venture, *The Mickey Mouse Club*.

Among the other future Mice whom Doreen eyed in the crowded commissary that day was Mary Espinosa, the kind of kid-next-door viewers could relate to. She was less of a showbiz kid than Doreen, though she did always have stars in her eyes. She felt like she just kept lucking into a performing career despite living in a place where most people couldn't afford a television, much less find themselves starring on it. She'd spent the previous few years crammed into an apartment at the Hansen Dam housing projects in the San Fernando Valley with her parents and six siblings—three older than her, three younger. A classic middle child, she craved attention, and she landed in dance class because of her parents' desperation to channel some of her hyperactivity into anything that would calm her down.

Ten years old at the time of her audition, she'd been studying dance since she was five and had landed a few previous TV jobs by chance. She ended up at auditions because the kid she'd carpooled with to dance class was always trying out for things, and she tagged along. When her friend would try out, the casting directors would often see Mary hovering nearby and ask if she'd like to audition, too. So at eight, she'd found herself in a small part on *The Loretta Young Show*. "I was a Girl Scout for one day and I got twenty-five dollars," she says. "So I had a résumé when they came around looking for the Mouseketeers. It was just enough to show I could take direction and someone had liked me enough to pay me."

Now here she was again, at an audition by happenstance. Her dance teacher, Burch Mann, had been hired to choreograph for *The Mickey Mouse Club*. So Mann had brought a handful of her students to the tryouts, including Mary. And when the hopeful faced her Disney judges, she did so without a twinge of nerves—maybe because it felt just like her regular dance class, maybe because she felt it was meant to be. Mary had spotted an article about the *Mickey*

Mouse Club auditions in her mom's *Reader's Digest* and, having relished her *Loretta Young* experience, had grown determined to be on the show. She knew she'd found her destiny when she saw that headline trumpeting, NEW CHILDREN'S SHOW! She showed it to her mother and told her, "I'm going to be on that."

Mann stood on the sidelines while Mary and some other girls from her class did a tap number they knew well. Piece of cake, just like any other dance-class day. Then one of the men at the table asked Mary to step forward and sing, and she belted out her favorite pop song, "Tweedlee Dee" without a care. "After that, they said I was in the first cut," she remembers. "That didn't mean much to me, but it meant a lot to my mom. It didn't matter as much to me because I just knew I was going to be on it. I don't know why I knew, I just did."

Carl "Cubby" O'Brien came to the same open casting call with a different talent: drumming. The tiny, eight-year-old suburban kid had learned his instrument from his dad, well-known pro drummer Haskell "Hack" O'Brien—and his skill made him a novelty among the Mouseketeer wannabes. "I started banging on everything in the house and my father decided I should take lessons," Cubby recalls. "After a few years I was getting pretty good. My grade school, Glenwood Elementary, was across the street from where we lived, and he asked the principal if he could come get me at lunchtime and take me home for a half-hour drum practice every day." Cubby joined the all-kiddie Roger Babcock Dixieland Band, a group made up of students from the studio where his dad taught. The Disney recruiters had spotted Cubby early in their scouting process, when he and the band played at a Christmas benefit—a show he'd almost missed due to a 103-degree fever. The scouts reported back to Walt Disney about the pint-sized group, and the boss then later caught the act on *The Ray Bolger Show* and requested that Cubby, its youngest member, audition for *The Mickey Mouse Club*. "I was flipping the sticks and playing drum solos," Cubby says, explaining his particular appeal. "I was eight but I looked like I was five or six."

Producers had first considered Cubby a possible onetime guest for Talent Round-Up Day, the show's theme day that would spotlight young performers, but then they saw a little blond girl from North Hollywood named Karen Pendleton and thought the two could make a cute matched set. The eight-year-old girl barely had more training than any average *Mickey Mouse Club* viewer might. She did, however, have some dance background and had ended up at the open audition with her dance teacher, Elaine Troy, and three other fellow students. "I took dancing lessons, and my dancing teacher had a friend who worked at Warner Brothers who saw it in *Variety* that there were auditions at Disney," she says. "So she took four of us. I had no idea what I was doing, but I would do anything a person of authority would tell me to do."

The youngest of three children, like Cubby, Karen excelled most at doing as she was told. She did just that during her audition, unaware anything out of the ordinary was even going on—to her, it could've been just another dance class. Though her father worked as a set builder, she'd had no show-business experience. She'd never even competed in an amateur contest or visited a professional set in her life. Her inexperience played to her advantage: Producers fell for her fresh innocence. And the show's adult host, Jimmie Dodd, was even more enchanted once he recognized her from a Sunday-school class at his church, the First Presbyterian Church of North Hollywood. She recognized him, too, which set her more at ease as she sang for the panel. Next thing she knew, Disney executives were calling her mother and telling her that her youngest daughter needed a work permit so she could report to the studio for duty.

Disney executives hoped Cubby would serve as Karen's male counterpart. "It just sort of evolved because we were the two smallest," Karen says. "They just thought we would look neat together," Cubby says. "I was a drummer—I didn't dance or sing—but when they thought of us together, they said, 'Can you start taking tap-dance lessons?' Luckily I picked it up real quick—because of the drums, I had rhythm, and as a little kid, you just absorb that stuff."

As for singing, Cubby squeaked by on his meager skills. At his final callback audition for Disney a few weeks after the open call, Jimmie asked the tiny boy if he could sing. Cubby, who'd thought he was all set once he'd learned to dance, replied, "I don't know."

Jimmie prodded: "Well, can you sing 'Happy Birthday'?" Cubby nodded and belted out the childhood-party staple, proving at least that he could carry a tune adequately. Producers sighed with relief. Besides loving the novelty of his instrumental talent paired with his tiny frame and the idea of matching him with the adorable Karen, they also thought his name—a nickname his mom gave him at birth because she thought he looked like a bear cub—couldn't be more perfect for Mouseketeerdom. He was in.

Bobby Burgess was as gifted a dancer as Cubby was a drummer, but when he first arrived at the mass audition from fifty miles away in Long Beach, he hadn't planned to show producers even one step. The lanky thirteen-year-old had won dozens of amateur talent contests, his extraordinary tapping and jitterbugging scoring him an impractical number of odd prizes. "I won four aquariums," he says, "and a bike. And washing machines. And watches."

But for this audition, he was planning to try his hand at acting instead, reading for a role on the in-the-works serial *The Adventures of Spin and Marty*, a short drama segment about two kids on a ranch that would run as a separate part of *The Mickey Mouse Club*. The story of the Triple R Ranch summer camp—which would consist of twenty-five episodes of about ten minutes each—was auditioning young actors so it could go into production at the same time as the Mouseketeer portion of the series, with its tryouts attracting almost as many young hopefuls as the Mouseketeer open call.

Bobby walked in ready to project confidence and charm as the laid-back Spin Evans, but the suited men to whom he thought he'd be reading quickly dimmed Bobby's permanent grin: "That part's already been cast," they told him. "But why don't you head across the way to the Mouseketeer auditions instead?"

Always up for anything, Bobby crammed into the commissary with the hundreds of other *Mickey Mouse Club* auditioners and waited his turn. A gifted dancer, he knew right away this could be his big break—a much better fit than being an actor, even though being on a ranch every day would've been cool. He looked around and saw the other kids tap-tap-tapping their way through pretty standard dance-class stuff—not that he thought he was better than they were or anything, just that he knew he was…different. He knew what he'd do for the producers. When they called his name and he entered yet another room to face yet another panel of suited men, he smiled that giant smile of his, then took off his shoes and socks.

He asked the piano player for "Rock Around the Clock," then launched into one of his bicycle-winning showstoppers—a barefoot jazz number—and knocked the producers' socks off. He and his parents would be making that fifty-mile drive every day for years to come. "After being in seventy-five amateur shows," he says, "I was ready for a job where I'd just be dancing. I wanted to pay my dues and get some professional experience."

When knockout singer Tommy Cole faced those same producers that day of the mass audition, the thirteen-year-old was shaking with nerves. He could sing anything in his clear soprano—he knew that much—but was terrified they'd ask him to dance. So many of the kids practicing out in the commissary were dancing—and to his untrained eyes, they were as good as Fred Astaire. He planned to compensate by doing his surefire act, a bit that often brought down the house at the local Pantages Theatre: singing "Mexicali Rose" while playing the accordion and wearing a sombrero. He hated the instrument, but how could they ask him to dance with that big keyboard strapped to him and his elaborate mariachi outfit on?

Though he'd played for radio shows and women's clubs, as he faced the producers' expectant eyes he felt a familiar gnawing in his stomach—the same kind of nausea that used to send him to the school nurse's office after any compulsory display of talent in music class. "She always knew I'd have to lie down for a while," he recalls. Yet he had found himself drawn to the stage anyway as he discovered he had the kind of talent that set him apart from other kids. Over time the acid in his belly disappeared with the freedom of singing. "Somehow entertaining in front of an audience of people I didn't know was a great catharsis for me. Where I might be shy talking to someone, onstage I wasn't shy anymore."

Just a few months before his *Mickey Mouse Club* audition, he had put his stage nerves to the ultimate test when he got a chance to sing "God Bless America" at the Rose Bowl in Pasadena. But those nerves were quieted when he won a key endorsement: He was rehearsing the patriotic ballad with a band at a nearby studio the day before his performance when none other than Bing Crosby happened by between recording sessions. Crosby stopped to watch as the boy belted it out, and when Tommy finished, the legendary crooner said, "Good voice." Then he walked out. Tommy could barely believe what had just happened to him.

So as Tommy's nerves were getting the better of him in that Disney Studios audition room, he reminded himself that *Bing Crosby* had noticed his singing. Not just noticed, but complimented! "I just thought, 'Man, Bing Crosby said I had a good voice!'" Tommy recalls.

The internal pep talks worked: "Mexicali Rose" wafted from his throat without a glitch, and the producers didn't ask him to dance a step. Instead, they asked Tommy back for a second go-round, to his relieved surprise. They did, however, have one parting request: "Come on back," they said, "but we don't want you to play accordion." His stomach dropped once again, worried the next round would be the dancing one. Then, to his relief, they added, "We just want you to sing." *That* he knew he could do.

But when he showed up for the callback, he got another surprise—they asked him to read on camera for a part in *Spin and Marty*. Unlike dancing, this prospect thrilled him. "I thought, 'This is cool, I really want this, to be able to go act and ride a horse and have a great time,'" he says. "I was sort of disappointed when I didn't get that part, but the reason they put me in the screen testing was they just wanted to see if I would freeze because I'd never really been on camera. I sang onstage in live performances, but had never really done anything on film."

After the reading, producers finally hit him with the request that he'd been fearing: He had to do a few quick dance steps, just to show them what he was (and wasn't) capable of. His performance was as weak as he'd feared—but their response wasn't. Charmed by his exceptional voice, they shrugged off his dismal tapping and ordered him to dance class with Burch Mann and Louis De Pron, who'd instructed several other soon-to-be Mice. "They put me into dance school, every night," he says. "Tap, jazz, ballet, anything where you see me in tights, it's not a pretty sight." Still, he was in. He was a Mouse. He never played the accordion again.

The *Mickey Mouse Club* cast still needed a few more exceptional dancers, so producers were itching to get a little girl named Sharon Baird. The tiny, Shirley Temple–esque dance prodigy had made memorable appearances on *The Colgate Comedy Hour* and *The Donald O'Connor Show* before she ran into host Jimmie Dodd at Capitol Records. She was in the Melrose Avenue building for an *Artists and Models* recording session; he was there cutting some *Mickey Mouse Club* records so they could hit store shelves just as the show premiered—and when he spotted her, he asked her if she'd consider trying out for *The Mickey Mouse Club*.

But her mother, protective of her daughter's burgeoning career, demurred. Soon casting director Lee Travers was on the phone making a personal plea to Sharon's agent. They wanted the dancing wunderkind. "My agent didn't want me to go out for the Mouseke-teers because she thought it would tie my schedule up," Sharon recalls. "So they said I could try out for this serial on the show called *What I Want to Be*, about a girl learning to be a stewardess and a boy learning to be a pilot, which would only be six weeks of filming."

That, her agent and mother could stomach.

But when the baby-faced, curly-haired Sharon showed up to read for *What I Want to Be*, it became obvious from the handful of other girls waiting there that she didn't quite look the part. "All the kids at those auditions had freckles and long hair with braids, and that was not me," Sharon says. "So when they called my name they said, 'Would you go down the street? We're auditioning for something else down there,' which was the Mouseketeers." Off she went to see *The Mickey Mouse Club* producers about a Mouseketeer spot.

Luckily Sharon had been dancing since she was three and, like Bobby, clearly belonged in production numbers, not scripted dramas. She'd studied with Hollywood dancer and choreographer Louis De Pron, and by just seven years old, her legs were insured for $50,000 by Lloyd's of London. By the time of her *Mickey Mouse Club* audition, she was twelve—and, naturally, she had a routine prepared that she'd been doing for years. The four-foot-eight-and-a-half-inch girl sang the Andrews Sisters' "I Didn't Know the Gun Was Loaded"—a Western-themed bit with a fancy tap routine involving tricks with a rope and dancing in double-time. Producers were so impressed, the routine would later be featured on the show itself. "My agent didn't want me to take it, but I wanted to," Sharon says. "My parents said if I wanted to do it, fine. If not, that's fine too. I just wanted to sing and dance every day, so I did it."

One of Sharon's old dance partners from *The Colgate Comedy Hour*, a boy named Lonnie Burr, came with a similarly impressive list of credits and so also managed to bypass the "cattle call" that brought so many kids together on that humid day in the commissary. The eleven-year-old liked to move fast and would add a bit of a cocky leading-man vibe to his role in the cast—at least as much as a preteen could. He was studying three years ahead of his grade level. His parents had brought him from Kentucky to Hollywood when he was three, and by age five he was embarking on a career in radio, movies, TV, theater, commercials, and modeling. He had seven films to his name pre–*Mickey Mouse Club*. And he was good, perhaps above all else, at touting his extensive experience. "I was working the business at five," he says. "I was working with huge stars, you know: Bob Hope, Martin and Lewis, Jimmy Durante."

Lonnie was reading for the part of snotty Marty Markham on *Spin and Marty*—but producers at that audition asked him, as they did Bobby and Sharon, to go out for the Mouseketeers instead. He resisted the idea at first—he heard the Mouseketeers would be making only the Screen Actors Guild minimum of $185 a week. "It bothered me because the guys on *Spin and Marty* were making so much more," he says. "My mom happened to be an agent at the time, and she happened to be *my* agent, so I knew."

The producers wanted Lonnie's poised stage presence and smooth dance skills for *The Mickey Mouse Club*, though, so they gave Lonnie's mom the hard sell. Lonnie ended up auditioning in a private room at the Disney Studios Animation Building, just as Sharon did, so he wouldn't have to endure the mass auditions, which were, as he saw it, strewn with amateurs. Just as he expected, he sailed through his tryout and earned a Mouseketeer contract offer. He says he didn't want to do it at first because he was also up for the lead role in CBS's *My Friend Flicka* series that would ultimately star Johnny Washbrook. "Mom and I agreed to refuse the Disney offer, and it did not help that no one knew for sure what in the hell the neologism 'Mouseketeers' was going to turn out to be," he writes in his memoir. "In addition, I had my own horse and had ridden since I was eight. Being a cowboy was definitely cooler than being a mousey something or other." But he says Disney producers pressured his mom, even going so far as to threaten that he'd "never work in Hollywood again" if he didn't take the gig. Whatever the reason, Lonnie, too, accepted a pair of Mouseketeer ears, still unsure of what he'd gotten himself into.

Like Lonnie and Sharon, two other future Mice sailed through auditions after being handpicked by producers, but for a different reason: Before the massive cattle call, Disney executives had picked out two early auditioners from a local dance studio. Producers visited ballet classes in Alhambra, just north of Los Angeles, run by choreographer Burch Mann, and plucked a little ten-year-old boy named Dallas Johann and fourteen-year-old Darlene Gillespie from the students there. Dancing had come naturally to Dallas, and when the Disney men who'd been scouting his class called him over and said, "How would you like to be on television?" the tiny boy didn't hesitate. "Like *The Little Rascals?*" he asked.

When they said yes, he was sold. "I guess they looked at me as the Alfalfa," Dallas recalls now. "I was very redheaded and freckle-faced. And I was tongue-tied as a child, too. I was in speech class all through preliminary school. But Disney thought it was cute." When Dallas came to Disney Studios to show the men how well he could dance and sing, they were sold.

Darlene Gillespie also had dancing in her blood and seemed an easy fit for the show-in-progress, albeit in different ways from little Dallas. The Canadian transplant, like Doreen the daughter of a former dance team, happened to also have a showstopping voice beyond her years. When her mom noticed the congregation tearing up while Darlene sang a solo in the church choir at age ten, the budding songbird got formal voice training without delay. After a while she added dance training to her résumé as well, studying with Mann.

When it came time to show the Disney executives she did, indeed, have what they were looking for, Darlene made the shrewd choice of the Disney smash hit "The Ballad of Davy Crockett" as her audition piece, cinching the deal. "I honest to God didn't do it like someone would say, 'What a sharp kid. She sang the favorite number,'" she said in a 1975 interview. "I sang it, honestly, because I really liked it. And I guess they liked it too." *The Mickey Mouse Club* would provide a chance for the world to at last partake of her God-given vocal gift.

Darlene and Dallas would become the first Mouseketeers—"guinea pigs," as Dallas remembers it, for camera setups and song trials. "I remember sitting outside the office at the Disney Studios and hearing Jimmie writing the songs for the show," Dallas says. "We were right there, Darlene and I, to actually hear the beginnings of this plan." After producers ran through some numbers with their first potential stars, "They gave both Darlene and me a two-week vacation. When they called us back, there were twenty-eight of us."

Walt Disney himself was responsible for finding just one Mouseketeer, one of the final additions to the bunch. He'd told his producers he wanted "ordinary kids" as Mouseketeers: "I don't want those kids that tap-dance or blow trumpets while they're tap-dancing or skip rope or have curly hair like Shirley Temple or nutty mothers." More than a few of those chosen ended up fitting that *exact* bill one way or another, in clear defiance of the boss's vision. While his idea seemed nice in theory, Walt, after all, wasn't the one who'd have to wrangle, choreograph, and direct these kids every day— and the producers, as such, chose several experienced, professional performers to anchor their cast.

But when Walt attended a dance-school recital during Easter week of 1955 at the Burbank Starlight Bowl, where his friend Leo Damiani was conducting the orchestra, he spotted her: that one kid with "star quality," as he'd explained it to producer Bill Walsh. "Go to a school and watch the kids at recess. Watch what happens to you. You'll notice that you're watching one kid. Not any of the other kids, but sooner or later your gaze will always go back to this one kid. That kid has star quality. Not a lot of star quality, maybe, but there's always a reason why you're watching that one kid. That's the kid we want to get in *The Mickey Mouse Club*."

She appeared during the ballet portion of the recital, a performance of *Swan Lake*. The Swan Queen pirouetted onto the stage in her ethereal white dress, a white feather headpiece setting off her short, dark curls, and Disney knew he'd spotted a star Mouseketeer. His studio executives called dance teacher Al Gilbert the next day to find out who she was.

And that's how twelve-year-old Annette Funicello—the daughter of Utica, New York, transplants named Joe and Virginia, who ran a filling station and had come to California for more sunshine—ended up on an unexpected track to the big time. Mr. Gilbert told Annette's mother the good news, that Mr. Walt Disney himself thought Annette could be a potential "Mouseketeer."

The term alone confounded Virginia. What on earth could her little girl have to do with anything involving musketeers? The Disney name, however, intrigued her a bit. Annette had loved *Snow White and the Seven Dwarfs*, *Cinderella*, *Pinocchio*, and especially *Bambi*. Still, Virginia would later recall, "We didn't know what an audition was, and who knew what a Mouseketeer was? We just didn't want to be bothered with it."

Mr. Gilbert persisted. "Look, to have Annette audition for Mr. Disney will definitely be a feather in my cap," he told Virginia. "Why don't you just go for the audition, and I'll come with you?" Annette would simply do a few dance routines, of which she knew many. Sweet-natured Virginia wanted to help Mr. Gilbert and figured the tryout would at least give her and her daughter a chance to see a movie studio, which could be fun.

Annette's Walt Disney approval put her on the fast-track audition process, skipping that mass audition the other kids had trudged through and going directly to the callback sessions. Even at that, the unusually wet Southern California weather on her audition day almost stopped her from showing up. "I wanted no part of it," she recalls in her autobiography, *A Dream Is a Wish Your Heart Makes*.

The shy preteen, used to the cocoon of a close-knit family and overprotective brothers, hated the idea of dancing on command, alone, in front of strangers who'd be judging her. But her mother promised Annette wouldn't have to do anything she didn't want to, and so Annette made the drive with Mom from their home in Studio City to the Walt Disney Studios in Burbank. The lack of glamour on the lot surprised Annette—this place had no more glitter than a school campus. Once inside, Disney security directed her and her mom to a room with other kids and their parents—all of them talking Hollywoodese about agents, contracts, and audition rounds. The whole scene wracked the polite girl's nerves, but she got through her ballet and tap numbers unscathed. "It's funny, but I'd noticed how my anxiety and shyness always just seemed to disappear when I danced," Annette wrote. "Well, maybe not disappear completely, but dancing and singing gave me a sense of joy that eclipsed everything else."

She repeated her audition drill through a few callbacks, gaining confidence with each one. Though things were going well, Annette panicked when Walt told her at her last tryout, "Okay, now, Annette, we'd like to hear you sing something."

"I'm sorry, Mr. Disney," she choked, "but I don't sing."

"Well, surely you can sing a few notes from one of your favorite songs," he reassured her.

After a deep gulp of air, she launched into Jaye P. Morgan's radio hit "That's All I Want from You."

Though none of the producers was overwhelmed by the star quality Walt insisted Annette had, that final audition—thanks, no doubt, to Walt's influence—was enough to get her the phone call she'd been hoping for: She'd be a Mouseketeer.

Annette, Doreen, Lonnie, Sharon, Darlene, Dallas, Cubby, Bobby, Karen, Tommy, Mary, and seventeen other kids would become the first official set of Mouseketeers. For most of those chosen, the decision to sign with Disney required little thought. "My parents tried to explain to me that I was going to be leaving my school and my friends, and I was going to go to Disney Studios," Cubby recalls. "Was this something I really wanted to do? I thought, 'Walt Disney? *Yeah*.' I used to go see all the animated movies. I waited for *Pinocchio* or *Cinderella*, whatever the new one was that was coming out. It sounded very cool to me." Adds Doreen, "I wanted it. I just *wanted* it."

On May 16, 1955, they signed contracts that would lock them into forty-eight-hour, Monday-through-Saturday workweeks. (By law, that included three hours of class time and one hour of recreation per day on the lot during the school year.) Even at the base rate, most of them were making more than their parents. The amount, however, meant less to the kids than the cachet of working for Walt Disney, an almost godlike figure to many families in the '50s. "The most fun thing was the checks, because they all had Mickey Mouse on them," says Mary. "My regret is that I didn't save one of those checks." Best of all, the chosen ones would now get to spend all of their days singing and dancing, the money incidental to the recognition of their talent. "I was so happy to have a job where I was just dancing my head off," Bobby recalls. "You see me the first year, I'm this wild, jitterbugging, extremely nerdy kind of guy. That's because I was just so happy to be there."

The idea that would give them such a life-changing opportunity, that would make those ordinary kids into icons, had started two years earlier as nothing more than a last-minute idea Walt Disney and his brother, Roy, had thrown together in a desperate plea for a cash infusion from the American Broadcasting Company. Yes, even Walt Disney found himself short on money sometimes—particularly when he was building what he hoped would be the greatest amusement park the world had ever seen. The show that would change children's entertainment started as nothing more than a way for Disney to drum up some quick funding for a much bigger dream—and even at that, it hadn't been ABC's first choice.

Chapter Three

The Making of a Hit

Roy Disney picked up the phone in his suite at New York City's Waldorf-Astoria Hotel and dialed Leonard Goldenson's office at ABC, hoping to reach the network chairman. Roy was in luck: Not only was Goldenson there, but he was willing to rush over to the hotel to meet with anyone named Disney. A good sign for Walt's business-minded brother, who'd taken the September 1953 trip across the country with a directive to wrestle a couple of million dollars from a television network to help finance plans to build a theme park. The brothers had struck out with the only two other networks, the far-more-powerful CBS and NBC. Goldenson and ABC represented their last chance at making a quick few million bucks in television.

As Roy prepared for the impending meeting, however, he fretted over the scantiness of the ideas he'd be offering ABC in return for the massive cash infusion. He held the six-page Disneyland project prospectus—fresh out of an airmail envelope rushed east from his brother back in Los Angeles—and turned to the single page that listed the possible television projects. Walt's greatest dream was on the line: He wanted to build an amusement park like no other. The Disneys had found box-office success with animated films such as *Peter Pan* and *Alice in Wonderland,* but it took a lot of cash to meet Walt's perfectionist standards, and it took even more to build a world-changing family tourist destination.

So the Disneys were reduced to begging for money, as they had so often done to build their empire over the last two decades. At least now they had their impeccable name to trade on: The idea was that they'd offer to give ABC some of their in-demand entertainment product in exchange for a stake in the park project. They'd planned to coast on their reputation so much, however, that they'd nearly forgotten to come up with *what,* exactly, they'd give to the network. While Roy headed to New York, Walt had stayed back home in Burbank to hammer out some last-minute TV ideas—and whip up some last-minute sketches of the park plans to show ABC executives.

The memo and the fresh plan renderings would arrive in Manhattan just in time, a huge relief, but when Roy opened the envelope, he faced another problem: The proposed television shows listed there were vague at best. The typed memo suggested a nature show; something called *World of Tomorrow,* which would document futuristic inventions; a series called *Disneyland* that would offer exclusive, behind-the-scenes looks at Disney films and the upcoming theme park; and a fifteen-minute broadcast live from Disneyland called *The Mickey Mouse Club,* modeled on the local fan groups that had sprung up at movie houses throughout the country back in the 1930s. That was it—no more than a few thought fragments, with little to no detail about their development or execution. Walt Disney, the man who'd taken four years to conceive *Snow White and the Seven Dwarfs*, gave his brother no more than a page-long, fragment-filled memo to mark the company's first foray into series television.

When Goldenson arrived at the Waldorf, Roy had nothing to do but hope for the best despite the haphazard nature of his preparations. "ABC was really Disney's last hope," Goldenson writes in his 1991 memoir. "He'd gone to the banks, and when he tried to explain what he wanted to build, they just couldn't grasp the concept [of Disneyland]. They kept thinking of a place like Coney Island. Very risky. They turned him down."

As it turned out, though, Goldenson—even though he knew Disney needed his network so badly—said yes almost before Roy could present the ideas to him. The fact was, the ABC chairman wanted to say yes to almost anything the Disneys had to offer. He wanted an hour-long, weekly show with the Disney name on it, whatever it might be. The brothers, caught up in their own desperation, hadn't realized ABC needed them as much as they needed ABC.

Goldenson had been trying to entice other film studios to sign deals with the network, but to no avail. Meanwhile, ABC's owner, industrialist Edward J. Noble, was rumored to be on the verge of selling Goldenson's whole operation to competitor CBS. The Disneys offered Goldenson a shot to prove ABC was still worth betting on. He struck a deal with the Disneys that amounted to a $5 million guaranteed loan, which would buy ABC a 35 percent interest in Disneyland the park. He'd have to convince his board of directors *and* finagle a complicated loan to get the money, but he was confident it would be worth it for the programming gold he'd get in return. "That's what I really wanted from them," Goldenson writes. The seven-year agreement, at $5 million annually, was then the biggest television package deal in history. "ABC needed the television show so damned bad," Walt Disney later said, "they bought the amusement park."

From the list of show possibilities, Goldenson plucked the one called *Disneyland*. The strongest of the memo's ideas—and the most similar to Disney's successful previous Christmas specials—the anthology concept dovetailed with his network's philosophy of targeting young families. Goldenson's gamble paid off: Kids and parents indeed gathered to watch the show together, drawn by the Disney name. The *Mickey Mouse Club* idea would lie buried in ABC's files for another year as *Disneyland* became the network's first big hit. But this first ABC–Disney collaboration would lay the groundwork for the kiddie sensation that would make stars out of two dozen unsuspecting young talents still toiling away anonymously in dance classes and school plays throughout suburban Los Angeles at the time.

When *Disneyland* debuted on ABC in 1954—the same year as the first color TV set and the first TV dinner—the show struck instantaneous success with its always-a-surprise mix of behind-the-scenes looks at Disneyland, construction footage from the sets of Disney movies such as *20,000 Leagues Under the Sea*, serialized dramas, and nature and science segments. It made a household name of Davy Crockett—and launched a national coonskin-cap craze—with its ongoing chronicles of the "king of the wild frontier."

"If the evening's promise is fulfilled in future weeks," the *New York Times*'s Jack Gould wrote, "the rest of the television industry may decide to suspend operations between 7:30 and 8:30 Wednesday nights." *Newsweek* called it "the first big-budget television show consistently and successfully aimed at the whole family."

There was plenty of cause for celebration as the network finally broke the top-25 on the Nielsen chart with *Disneyland*. But CBS and NBC still dominated the ratings to an embarrassing degree. ABC's weakness was a matter of sheer mathematics: It had fourteen affiliates to NBC's sixty-three and CBS's thirty, with much lower advertising rates as a result. Ironically, *Disneyland*'s success had brought even more pressure to bear on Goldenson, rather than relieving it: Now that he'd found a hit despite the market forces that worked against his fledgling network, the board believed more hits were possible. And it wanted more as soon as it could get them.

Goldenson and his network president, Robert Kintner, knew they needed a fresh blockbuster to keep ABC's new momentum going. As ABC's number-six *Disneyland* sat above NBC's *The Bob Hope*

Show but below CBS's *Toast of the Town* and four other shows, they thought back to how they had dug themselves out of near-extinction the previous year—and they dug up the Disney memo. They looked at the old Disney pitch list for any other idea that could be viable. Skipping right over the nature show and *World of Tomorrow*, they landed on the one remaining concept. Described there as a mere fifteen-minute broadcast with few other details, *The Mickey Mouse Club* nonetheless sparked something in the ABC suits.

They wanted a competitor to NBC's *Howdy Doody*, TV's oldest children's programming at the time, on the air since 1947. ABC also needed something to go head-to-head at five p.m. against *The Pinky Lee Show*, which featured a former burlesque comic as a clowning children's show host. (His catchphrase: "Yoo, hoo, it's me! My name is Pinky Lee!")

This *Mickey Mouse Club* series idea could fill that need, if fleshed out the right way. For starters, the fifteen-minute broadcast proposed on the memo would not do the job—why not a full hour, five days a week? Aglow with the possibilities, Kintner wrote Disney to buy the new series gushing—with hints of both wild flattery and, perhaps, hopeful thinking—that it would have "the potential for the highest-rated show in the daytime; for the greatest impact on children in the history of communications; and for the creation of a product that not only will have the enthusiastic support of parents, Parent Teacher Associations, etc., but will bring a new dimension to daytime programming." Who better than Disney—whose *Disneyland* had proven the "turning point" for the network, according to Goldenson—to provide ABC such a momentous series? Kintner granted Disney "absolute creative control"—which meant it would be up to Walt and his studio to come up with the particulars that would fill these five hours of kiddie television each week.

The offer intrigued Walt Disney right away, but he was skeptical of his studio's ability to produce so much TV. (He'd proposed *The Mickey Mouse Club* as a fifteen-minute show for a reason; the studio had a hard enough time making one hour of TV a week for *Disneyland*, let alone five extra hours a week.) But Disney was also no fool—a visionary with an intuitive feel for the budding consumerism taking over America, he knew this kind of marketing stunt would drive kids and their parents to buy tickets to Disneyland. So in the end, he took the chance to get more airtime. If TV could sell dishsoap to housewives, it seemed a fair assumption it could sell amusement and entertainment to kids.

Because the endeavor would also represent a shift for Disney, from animated works that transcended age to kiddie-focused fare, he wanted to keep the standards high. "We're not going to talk down to the kids," he told his staff. "Let's aim for the twelve-year-old. The younger ones will watch, because they'll want to see what their older brothers and sisters are looking at. And if the show is good enough, the teenagers will be interested. Adults, too."

He tasked producer Bill Walsh with executing this tricky new concept. With television still in its infancy, Walsh stood among the few experienced producers around, having handled both the first Disney Christmas special and *Disneyland*. Disney had promoted him from press agent to television pioneer when he ran into Walsh on the studio lot one day and barked, to Walsh's surprise, "You! You be the producer of TV." When Walsh told Disney he didn't have the experience, Walt replied, "Who does?" Walsh learned quickly, though, and subsequently built a reputation in those early television endeavors for getting things done while keeping Walt Disney happy.

Now, with a whole new TV venture to launch, Walt cornered his favorite producer once again. Walsh, exhausted from the first season of producing the weekly *Disneyland* and hoping to request some vacation time soon, had just said to his boss, "Boy, you know, I didn't think we'd get through that first year [of *Disneyland*]. We were used to doing an hour every three to five years for animation, but doing a show every week, that was murder." So it was with a hearty dose of trepidation that he listened as Walt laid out his hopes for *The Mickey Mouse Club*. "An hour every day?" Walsh asked, stunned. "Yes," Disney answered. "With children." With that, Walt gave Walsh some notes to work with—vague snippets like "mouse party," "special shows acted by children in Disneyland," "gadget band," "kids participate," "honor Sunday-school teachers," and "everyone can sing." Walsh would never get his vacation.

Arranging such fragments into a cohesive show that Disney would approve posed even more challenges than making *Disneyland* had. Walsh and his staff came up with a cast of characters for *The Mickey Mouse Club* that included a master of ceremonies, a musician, and a talking mynah bird, with children only as guests and studio audience members, but it just felt like standard kids' fare. Walt balked, complaining that it didn't meet his originality standards.

Then, after two months of futile brainstorming, inspiration struck: Instead of adults making up *The Mickey Mouse Club* company, why not kids? Real ones, playing themselves? A Disney Studio memo soon thereafter deemed the kids "Mouseketeers" for the first time, instructing, "get costumes, sweaters, little hats," and declared, "audience not necessary, just kids." Another note from Walt coined a funny-sounding variation: "The younger, less talented kids, who are still amateurs, will be called MEESKETEERS." Now Disney indeed had a game-changing concept: Kids—lots and lots of kids—as TV variety show stars.

The kids would need some adult guidance onscreen, though, and when producers started looking for those two adults who would set the tone for the entire show—whom they dubbed "Mooseketeers"—they were lucky enough to find a duo of real-life characters as colorful as cartoons, who would end up making the most memorable contributions yet to the show. "We were looking for talent wherever we could find it," Walsh would recall later. "We were grabbing the janitor right off his broom. I was going after everything and nothing."

First Walt himself recruited Roy Williams, who had come up through the Disney ranks during the golden age of animation in the '30s and '40s, developing a reputation as not so much the most talented artist as one of the funniest. One day, as Roy toiled away on *The Mickey Mouse Club*'s storyboards, Walt blurted out to the robust barrel of a fellow, "Say, you're funny-looking. I'm going to put you on the show and call you the Big Mooseketeer." When Roy protested that he didn't know how to sing or dance—and anyone who watched the show knows he wasn't kidding—Walt told him not to worry about it. "That just shows you again the genius of Walt Disney," Roy said in a 1976 interview. "Walt knew I loved kids and people even before I knew it. That's why he put me on a kids' show. I'm a down-to-earth guy, but I never dreamed of the kind of pleasure that working with those kids brought me."

From the music department the producers plucked redheaded songwriter and onetime actor Jimmie Dodd, a forty-five-year-old known best for penning the official song of Washington, D.C. At first they'd asked him just to come up with a few tunes for the new series. But soon enough, Walsh realized the born-again Christian music man with the perma-smile would make a perfect Mooseketeer partner for Roy. But he also knew Walt had to feel he'd been the one to discover him, and so he engineered a meeting in which Jimmie would sing for the head honcho. Once Jimmie performed his song about an animated pencil, Walt came in on cue: "Hey, Jim is the one who should be on *The Mickey Mouse Club*!" Walsh knew his Walt Disney.

It wasn't, however, until Jimmie and Roy started brainstorming their own ideas for the show that Walsh knew just how valuable his new hires would be. In one of their first meetings, Roy offered an offhand suggestion: Always the consummate animator, he remembered a cartoon in which Mickey "tipped" his ears, hat-style, at Minnie. Maybe, he proposed, that would make a cute cap for the Mouseketeers. Jimmie, meanwhile, showed up at a session with a freshly composed little ditty, a song he'd just whipped up for possible use on the show, a simple tune with a marching beat that revolved around spelling out M-I-C-K-E-Y M-O-U-S-E. It was, they had to admit, catchy.

With those key elements and a cast of twenty-eight kids in place, *The Mickey Mouse Club* was born. Plenty of questions, however, remained: Would viewers think it was as visionary as ABC did? Would dozens of singing, dancing children wearing mouse ears be cute—or creepy? And how on earth would producers wrangle more than a classroom's worth of mostly amateur, sometimes rambunctious, and seldom predictable preteens and teenagers into filming a daily television show?

Chapter Four

A Phenomenon Is Born

Four of the happiest kids you've ever seen, wearing funny caps with ears on them and their names across their white sweaters in big black letters, emerged from behind the curtain that said MOUSEKETEERS. As the blue velvet parted between the giant pictures of a smiling boy and girl, the kids tap-danced to a hyper-jazzy tune as if their lives depended on it. Three more joined them in perfect time. The last three to join were tinier, younger, their dancing not as perfect as the others, but what they lacked in dance skill they made up for in cuteness.

Finally, a tall, skinny man named Jimmie (according to his sweater) and a round, bald one named Roy came out to lead the group in a rousing sing-along: "We Are the Merry Mouseketeers." When they finished the song, Jimmie sang out "Roll Call!" and they lined up in perfect straight-line formation to introduce themselves one by one: "Karen! Johnny! Sharon! Mike! Nancy! Lonnie! Darlene! Don! Doreen! Bobby! Annette! Roy! Jimmie!" At the end came the Mouseketeers' unofficial battle cry: "Yay!"

That's what the millions who tuned in to ABC to witness Walt Disney's latest TV creation saw the first time they laid eyes on the Mouseketeers on October 3, 1955. And just like that, most every child in America knew that a Mouseketeer had nothing to do with a musketeer, that only the coolest kids wore hats with little black ears protruding from them, and that Mickey Mouse could be spelled out in a rhythmic cadence. They watched, rapt, through the three-minute-long "Mickey Mouse Club March" opening, through newsreel reports about speedboats on the Everglades and behind-the-scenes looks at the upcoming serial *Spin and Marty*, through "The Shoe Song" featuring Mouseketeers dancing in different shoes (ballet, tennis, tap) as Roy sketched them and a *What I Want to Be* segment about a boy who hoped to be a pilot and a girl who hoped to be a stewardess. Audiences' eyes remained glued to the television screen all the way through until the reflective closing number, "The Mickey Mouse Club Alma Mater": From now on, parents would know *exactly* where their children were between five and six p.m. every weekday evening.

The show that had begun as a sketchy idea on a last-minute memo two years earlier became an instant smash. The show's premiere episode garnered more viewers during the hour than NBC and CBS combined. ABC president Robert Kintner wired Walt Disney from New York, thrilled with the results of the network's second collaboration with him: "I saw *The Mickey Mouse Club* and enjoyed it, and if my friends and acquaintances, including my six-year-old and twelve-year-old, are an indication, the show should go very well." Indeed, millions of kids joined the Club from their own homes by sending in for official membership cards. Mouseketeer hats (retail price: 69 cents) became the Disney empire's best-selling item over the next several years, peaking at twenty-four thousand a day. Bubble-bath sets, "Mousegetars," Mouseketeer dolls, and more than two hundred other kinds of merchandise helped fulfill fans' insatiable need for *Mickey Mouse Club* gear.

But the kids who'd become instant icons and symbols of '50s perfection weren't always as perfect—or always as happy—as they looked while tapping their hearts out on the Mouseketeer stage. Their harried producers were under so much pressure that the stress often trickled down to their charges. "We would discuss an idea in the morning," producer Bill Walsh recalled. "The songwriters would write songs that day, and we would shoot in the afternoon. It was probably the quickest draw on television." In fact, getting the show ready to air had been a monumental struggle—worse than the hardest algebra test or Little League game the Mouseketeers' fans could imagine—against its stars' youthful insecurities, inexperience, and natural troublemaking tendencies. Keeping the show going would prove a constant test of the producers' organization, crowd control, and patience—and of the Mouseketeers' drive, discipline, and ability to keep from crying while cameras were rolling.

Five months before the Mouseketeers' TV debut, Paul Petersen sat with his grandmother in the back of a stuffy cab as it drove under the iron archway announcing the Walt Disney Studios' entrance. The nine-year-old was among the twenty-eight kids starting work that spring day in 1955 as the cast of *The Mickey Mouse Club*. He had already been on the Disney lot a few times before to audition for the new show, but it felt different this time, knowing he was there as one of the stars, not just as some kid who wanted to be one. Then again, some of those other kids at the tryouts had been awfully good singers and dancers—what if once Paul got inside, Mr. Disney realized it had been a big mistake hiring him? What if Mr. Disney took it back? As the cab pulled up to the little house at the gate, a policeman-type asked for a name. When Paul's grandma told the uniformed man, "Paul Petersen," the boy felt good again. It was *his* name that was on that list, not his grandma's, not any other adult's. He belonged there.

The man shuffled his papers and scrunched his face as he looked for Paul on his list. The longer it took, the more Paul went right back again to realizing he was no star. Surely *Sky King*'s Kirby Grant and *Davy Crockett*'s Fess Parker didn't have to tell anyone their names at any gates. Paul sweated in the unusually hot late-spring sun, squirming in his seat; the ride over was boring, but this waiting was even worse. He wondered if any of the other kids had to come in a cab or with their grandmas—his parents both worked at Lockheed, so they couldn't come with him or even drive him. His family had to get a babysitter to watch his two sisters, a twelve-year-old and a seven-month-old, so his grandma could come with him here. They had to reschedule everything just to get him to be on this show, so he hoped he'd do okay at it.

Finally, the guard found Paul's name on the list and directed them through the gate. The cab cruised through the cooling shade of Mickey Avenue's trees, passed the Inking & Painting Department and the Camera Building, toward Dopey Drive. As he looked at the little outlines of cartoon characters on the iron signs, Paul thought about being a Mouseketeer, wondering what he and the other kids would be doing every day. He figured it would be a lot like auditions, with singing and dancing and stuff like that, but he didn't really know. He did know this place was really pretty, with lots of green grass and all kinds of flowers, like the nicest park. That made him feel better.

The cab let Paul and his grandma out at a big building called Sound Stage 1. They found relief from the hot day by stepping inside the cool, dark, warehouselike room that smelled of freshly constructed sets—lumber and paint—and echoed their voices back to them off cement walls. Paul and his grandma joined his fellow Mice and their parents in marveling at the overwhelming combination of the showbizzy (lights and cameras!) and the familiar (Mickey and Minnie!).

The overall atmosphere on the lot stunned many a kid among the producers' more untrained picks: Paul and his grandma, for instance, had no idea that there was a building on the lot called a commissary—a cafeteria—where they'd be able to eat all their meals. "We brought a bag lunch and sat on the grass until Tommy

Cole's mom, Junebug [June Olsen Cole], finally said, 'Why don't you go to the commissary?'" Paul says. "That's how astonishing it all was."

Mary Espinosa couldn't believe her luck either: "The best thing was to get out of county housing and into a group of kids who were phenomenal, to be treated like one of them. It was almost unbelievable. In the first month I kept having to pinch myself."

As the producers gathered the kids and started to rehearse some numbers that first day, though, the stark reality of competition cut through the fairy-tale atmosphere on the set. It began, of course, with the parents—not the kids. The mothers stood just behind the Disney crew and stage-whispered instructions to their offspring: "Smile!" "Louder!" They would see one kid doing a special number and complain to the producers, "My daughter should be doing this." A handful of offenders became a major nuisance, yelling at their own kids to upstage the others. "Move over," they'd command their darlings, "you're letting that other person in!" The producers, already under enough pressure to make the complicated production work, couldn't tolerate the extra interference. "That was the tough part," production coordinator Hal Adelquist would say in a 1977 interview, "dealing with the pushy mothers."

By the second day of shooting, producers banished the mothers and other on-set guardians—known together as the "Mousekemoms," though that included Darlene's dad and Lonnie's aunt Pud—to the theater across the way from the soundstage. "The parents were kept in the movie theater from then on," Cubby explains.

"They would do their card-playing and knitting, and [Disney] would show movies there for them while we worked. They weren't allowed on the set unless they were invited on the set. Which happened, occasionally." Adds Lonnie, "They could have lunch with the kids, and the kids could come talk to them. But not having them on the set, that was wise."

Disney even bought a TV set and sewing machines for the mothers to use while they waited. Pesky child labor laws required this sort of elaborate parent management system on a show that employed such a large number of kids: Every kid had to have a designated guardian on set, though moms would take liberties with the two-child-per-adult loophole, leaving their progeny under temporary care of another mom while they flitted off on a few errands. Many of the Mousekefamilies had to rearrange every part of their home lives—no easy task—to adhere to this rule. The Funicellos, for instance, had to drop off Annette's two-year-old brother, Michael, to stay with his godmother every day, as Annette's father worked six days a week running his garage in Sherman Oaks. "Poor Michael cried almost all day long, which broke my mother's heart," Annette writes. "Siblings and other children weren't allowed on the lot—for insurance reasons, I understand—so she really had no choice."

Still, the sequestering of the Mousekemoms didn't erase the growing tension over the differentials in talent among the Mice. The kids started to separate into two groups: the star players and, well, the others. "You've got to do the lines, hit the mark, do it in the first take, otherwise they'll say, 'We have to move on here,'" Lonnie says. "And, you know, it's a difficult thing for kids to do. I did all right, but I had been doing it. I was trained."

Soon enough, a group rotation system developed. Disney executives presented it as nothing more than a practical division—one group of Mouseketeers could be shooting while another rehearsed and another attended classes, as required by law, in the school trailers on the lot. But the system was really a thinly veiled hierarchy meant to keep the Mice (and the Mousekemoms) in line. The dozen or so members of the "Red Team"—Sharon, Bobby, Lonnie, Annette, Darlene, Cubby, Karen, and Doreen, as well as a few other fluctuating additions and subtractions—were the defacto starting lineup (the ones who'd appear in the trademark Roll Call at the beginning of each episode and in the singing of the "Alma Mater" at the end). The White and Blue Teams served as the second string. Those two six-member groups handled some intros, served as the "audience" during the less-popular Guest Star Day and Circus Day, and dressed in costume as background players in skits that highlighted the Red Team. "I was in costume ninety percent of the time," Blue-Teamer Mary says. "I was a kitty cat, I was a fat lady in the circus, I was a strong man in the circus."

Promotions and demotions could come at any time. For instance, producers shunted one of their earlier favorites, Dennis Day, off to the Blue Team when they discovered he couldn't sing. He had charmed the audition panel when he and his sister, who were performing a dance routine together, were thrown by the pianist playing off tempo. The twelve-year-old took charge, stopping the music to sort things out—and impressing the producers so much with his confidence that they offered him a job on the spot. They, however, forgot one thing in the excitement of the moment and the mayhem of mass auditions: They never asked the kid to sing. When filming started and they found out he couldn't carry a tune, he got booted to the second string. As he explained in a 1971 interview, the White and Blue Teams "were the ones that got stuck in the 'we need a body here' trips. If you got taken off the Red Team and put on one of the others, that was the handwriting on the wall." The downgrade could result from a poor performance or an over-the-line stage parent's outburst or even just a producer's or director's whim. "I think there was a lot of jealousy and a lot of strife, but we didn't talk about it," Blue-Teamer Mary recalls. "There were hurt feelings. 'Why can't *we* go to some event or party [with the Red Team kids]?' It was just the way it was, but the older kids, especially, knew they were being left out of certain things."

Even the Red-Teamers couldn't relax into complete security: "There was a pecking order from the beginning," Doreen says. "Who can do a slide right, who can do a triple-time step and jump over their leg at the same time." Many of them—Annette included—remained petrified of performing for others, despite their early experiences with local audiences. Those more bashful cast members retreated further into their shells as they observed some of their more overtly talented costars. "When performed by Sharon," Annette writes, "even the most athletic, complex tap maneuvers looked simple—until you tried them yourself." Differences in skill level grew before their eyes: Sharon ended up in almost every musical number, often paired with Lonnie or Bobby, the only two male dancers up to the challenge.

Darlene, in particular, was already pulling out way ahead of the rest of the Mice. She was the obvious teachers' pet, a favorite of producers and casting directors because of her golden voice and uncanny poise. She had featured prominently in several musical segments the Mice had already filmed. And shortly afterward she was shipping off for a few weeks to Big Bear Lake, about one hundred miles east of Burbank in the San Bernardino National Forest, to star in her very own serial drama segment, *Corky and White Shadow*. The story of a girl and her dog helping to solve an Old West bank robbery, it was created just for her to go along with *The Adventures of Spin and Marty* and *What I Want to Be*. Producers felt she needed a showcase as soon as possible. Gawky but pretty, all strawberry-blond waves and teeth, she looked the part of an accessible star to whom regular kids could relate, the way producers figured it.

She was also a whip-smart overachiever who attacked her first "leading role" with serious determination—and proved, over time, to have a sarcastic edge and a Joan Rivers–esque knack for dry wit, with hints of Carol Burnett–style physical-comedy skill. Soon Disney asked her to record the songs from the company's hit animated film *Alice in Wonderland*, for a special 1956 album; it would go on to sell for the next four decades on the strength of her voice.

Not even her costars bothered to deny she was the standout of the entire group. "So much possibility," Doreen says. Adds Mary, "She was my best friend on the show, and I was so proud of her. She had a magnificent operatic voice and also was a wonderful actress."

But her strong personality and single-minded career focus made her a love/hate proposition among her castmates. "Darlene was so smart," says Doreen, an early friend and admirer of Darlene's. "She was working her butt off. She wanted to do everything just right." Adds Karen, "Darlene was a riot. So funny, so talented." Lonnie, however, was among those who felt differently: "She certainly was a very good singer, I'll say that. But we always had problems. She's one of those people who's obsessed with being the center of attention. Just because you're a damn good singer doesn't mean you need to be like that." Her undeniable voice caused other singers to bristle at their stiff competition too. "There were two singers on the show: Darlene and me," Tommy says. "Wherever there were male solos, I got them. And Darlene, same thing with the female solos. But with specialty numbers, I'd get it *or* she'd get it. There was a little jealousy between the two of us the first year."

As the time came to transition from rehearsals to shooting the actual show, another jolt came when the uniforms materialized: strange beanies with big, round, black ears sticking out of either side and sweaters with the Mouseketeers' first names in giant stitching. Despite all the surprises of the past few weeks, these outfits may have come as the biggest shock. Many of the cast members couldn't get past the cookie-sized ears made of felt with wire inside to hold them up (unlike those later sold to the public, which had cheaper plastic appendages): "Too goofy!" the Mouseketeers said upon seeing them. "Who are they kidding? I'm not wearing this!" Annette wondered about those sweaters, too. "I thought, 'How are we going to get away with wearing our names across these?'" she writes. "It seemed so silly." The kids still remained unclear about what a Mouseketeer even was and what made them one—but apparently it involved wearing a uniform unlike anything the world had ever seen.

When the cameras arrived to start shooting the show—they would tape months ahead of the premiere date to stay on top of the rigorous daily airing schedule—their presence flummoxed some of the younger Mice in particular. "The first time we were performing a number, all of a sudden in the middle of it, the director goes, 'Cut!'" Karen recalls. "I thought he was crazy. Why would he stop us in the middle? I thought we were live on television."

Dallas soon became an unexpected problem as film started to roll: Although producers had chosen him as an early Mouseketeer with Darlene and had tried out some of their material ahead of time with the young boy, they hadn't ever thought to try it *on camera*. Every time the all-quiet bell rang on set to signal the start of shooting and the director pointed at Dallas—even for something as simple as saying his own name during a practice Roll Call sequence—he cried. "They went by height down the row," says Dallas, who was the second shortest boy in the bunch. "This made it even worse for me because they started with the tallest. I was in tears before they even got to me. They were all showbiz kids, and that intimidated me."

Making matters worse, the tongue-tied speech impediment that producers had found so adorable when they'd auditioned Dallas was now freezing him up onscreen. He couldn't help comparing himself with Cubby, who beat him at being the smallest Mouseketeer—by a half inch—and stood out because of his drumming. "All I saw were these wonderful, talented children who could do everything I could do but much better," Dallas says, "and *they* didn't get scared." He felt alone in his struggles, having lost the one fellow Mouseketeer friend he had, Darlene, first to the Red Team and then to her faraway location shoot for *Corky and White Shadow*. He had no parent on set with him to help boost his confidence—his mother worked as a private secretary, so Cubby's father would often serve as Dallas's guardian. But Mr. O'Brien often found himself taking Dallas—coincidentally enough, his son's closest competition—out to the Disney Studios lawn to teach him drumming techniques while producers gave all the prime little-boy parts to Cubby. Dallas was a willing victim, however, desperate to get out of camera range: "Cubby was getting everything, but I wouldn't have been able to do it anyway. Mr. O'Brien was doing me a favor."

Now producers were forced to try to smooth over their audition oversights. During the musical numbers Dennis appeared in, for example, they begged him not to sing aloud: "For God's sake, Dennis, *mouth* it!" Meanwhile, they continued to try to ease Dallas into working on camera. They'd dress him in traditional Chinese garb with a large hat covering his face or put him in the background as several Mouseketeers admired a new baby colt onscreen, hoping his relative obscurity would calm him down. They would use him and other Blue and White Team members to test out scenes that would, in the end, go to the Red Team when it was time to shoot, and Dallas had no problem with that since cameras weren't rolling. Jimmie would try to boost the boy's spirit with compliments, assuring him, "Nobody can outdance you." Dallas, however, always had a hard-to-dispute comeback: "Well, you know, Bobby can...."

Despite those early jitters, however, the kids started to settle into their new soundstage home and their Mouseketeer roles. The producers, as they got to know the kids, would sometimes incorporate the cast's own backstage antics into skits: "One time late at night when we got the giggles, Annette and I had written a song with our little patty-cake thing and the director saw it and pulled us out and filmed it," Sharon remembers, then sings: " '*We are two merry Mouseketeers, as merry as can be, and when we start to wiggle our ears we jump and laugh with glee.*' " They'd also keep mistakes in the routines sometimes to show that the Mice were regular kids, rather than reshooting after every misstep. "They would capitalize on my mistakes, which they thought was great but I thought was not nice," Karen says. "At least they were laughing with me and not at me, but still."

Producers would work the best of the kids' own routines, the ones they had auditioned with, into the show or allow them their own special moments in other ways: "I did several shows [including one that would run premiere week] where my dad and brother were on and we did a drum thing together," Cubby recalls. "That was a big thrill." In fact, Cubby, as the cast's lone musician, had an entire backing band at his disposal so that he could show off his unique instrumental skills. "They had a Dixieland band at the studio," he says. "They weren't really professional, but they were really good players. They were called the Firehouse Five Plus Two, a seven-piece band. They came on the show so I could do numbers with them. It was real fifties, new swing music kind of stuff."

The Mice could even occasionally get away with the tiniest bit of clowning around on set, though it was hard to know just how far they could go. Karen, usually well-behaved, acted out a restless urge by sticking chewing gum in Cubby's hair during a special *Fantasia* screening in the theater where their moms spent their days. "I just thought it would be really funny to be a little mischievous," Karen recalls, "but afterwards, it wasn't." Their parents had to cut the sticky wad out of her onscreen dance partner's hair—and were none too pleased about the bald spot it left (one thing Mouse ears were good for).

Sometimes the goofing bordered on disastrous, like the time Darlene went up to the sound booth and yelled into the microphone just to hear her own voice boom through the speakers, rattling even the usually patient director Dik Darley, who was feeling pressured as the premiere date neared. "She was just clowning around," Tommy recalls. "But Dik Darley was really upset with her." She felt terrible for having stressed him out even more: "Even though we were young," Tommy says, "we knew we had to be professional."

Another time, Dennis found a vial of stage blood in a makeup box, smeared it all over his arm, and ran up to Darlene to scare her. He didn't realize she was talking to none other than Mr. Disney. "*He* really freaked until I managed to explain the whole thing," Dennis recalled. "Then he just looked disgusted and walked away."

The Mice were also starting to warm to their cohost Mooseke-teers, Roy Williams and Jimmie Dodd. The doofy, fun-loving Roy would tell an occasional dirty joke and, according to some Mouse accounts, ask the kids to help him hide the odd bottle around the soundstage. "He was a funny, funny guy," Tommy says. "Every now and again a little snide remark would come out, maybe a little off-color, but we all loved him to death. Nobody was offended. He was that type of personality where he'd say a little something under his breath, but no one minded."

If Roy was the mischievous devil sitting on the kids' left shoul-der, Jimmie was the angel on the right. "He would never yell at anyone," Cubby says. "It wasn't in his personality." The lead Mouseketeer took his job seriously—particularly his responsibility to the children he performed alongside. "He just made the whole thing so easy and he treated everybody exactly the same whether you were Annette or whether you were somebody that nobody was ever going to hear of again," Cubby says. "He just had this way of treating everybody the same and with respect and love. He was a great person to be around as a kid."

Bobby reveled in the constant questions about whether he and Jimmie—who had similar peaks of brownish-red hair and crescent smiles that took up half of their animated faces—were related. "He was a close confidant," Bobby says, noting how much he relished the resemblance. "I was proud to call him a friend of mine." Tommy, who used to practice his champion chess skills with Jimmie, and Lonnie, never one to be easily impressed, looked up to the lead Mouseketeer too, and would later credit his influence with keeping them out of typical child-star trouble. "Jimmie was like a big brother," Tommy says. "He was a big influence, I think, on the viewing audience, and a very big influence on us as kids." As Bobby says, "He was one of the reasons the show was such a success. It was the right guy for the right time."

The Mice were getting comfortable with each other, the adults around them, and the set that would be their home away from home up to six days a week from now on. They were finally hitting their stride several weeks into taping, with a few months still to go before their premiere date.

Then Mice started disappearing from Sound Stage 1.

A few weeks into production, Jimmie pulled Dallas onto his lap for what would turn out to be his final talk with the terrified nine-year-old. "We know how this upsets you, being here on camera," the gentle Mooseketeer said. "We think it would be better if you don't have to do it anymore." The boy smiled, relieved. "I felt free," Dallas remembers. "I felt like I was serving a life sentence in prison and I got out."

Producers at once swapped his eleven-year-old brother, John Lee, into Dallas's place, having spotted him in the same dance class as Dallas once upon a time. "They'd picked me because I was more cute," Dallas says. "My brother was not freckled, and he was a year and a half older. But he also wasn't shy, and he wasn't tongue-tied." John Lee had mixed feelings about taking his brother's spot: "I was hurt that I didn't get it originally," he says. He would've been thrilled to finally be asked to take part in *The Mickey Mouse Club*—except it meant working *without* his brother. "We were very close," he says. "We danced a lot together, so it was unusual for us to be apart."

Thus one of the first to be cast became the first to be fired (though there are conflicting claims to that dubious honor). "I was the Unknown Mouseketeer," Dallas says, since he appeared in only a few hard-to-spot background roles to be caught on camera and aired. Dallas had just one moment of regret about leaving *The Mickey Mouse Club* behind: "I asked if I could have my ears," he says. "When they said no, I was devastated." (He'd go on to a surprisingly long performing career for the kid who once could do nothing but cry on cue, getting steady work as a chorus member in several Elvis Presley movies, helping to choreograph several Rat Pack movies, serving as an onscreen double for the likes of Gene Kelly, and appearing in a slew of Broadway productions in the late '60s and early '70s.)

Paul Petersen—who, despite Dallas's story, calls himself "the first ex-Mouseketeer" in his memoir *Walt, Mickey, and Me*—was having his own problems facing what he saw as an enormous gulf between himself and some of the more talented standouts of the cast. "It's funny, even at that young age, you know who the good dancers are, you know who the good singers are," he recalls. "I had incredible admiration for Tommy Cole as a singer; he was wonderful. Watching Bobby Burgess dance was fantastic; it was like watching Gene Nelson or Fred Astaire. He was much older than the rest of us, and he effortlessly learned the routines, helped the younger kids get their act together. And then you say, 'Okay, where do I fit in this group?' And I was so small. I was Cubby-sized."

Paul was among the handful of original chosen Mice who, though they'd aced their auditions, just didn't have the right temperament for Mousehood—because they were still, at their core, *regular* kids. "It quickly came to pass that I obviously didn't know much about discipline," he remembers. "But it was just so intriguing—I mean, it was the Disney Studios. You walked around and the paint shops were open and the little ladders led up to the top of the stages. How cool was that? It was paradise for a nine-year-old. So right away I earned a reputation—and well-deserved—as a kind of discipline problem. I could do the work, that wasn't any problem, and if it required some athletic ability, whether it was a gymnastics routine or something silly that required some physical skills, well, I just threw myself right into it. But this problem of not being where I was supposed to be persisted. You know, they'd call, 'Where's Paul?' and I'd holler from the top of the stage, 'I'm up here!' Not what you want in a supposed professional. And as I explain to people, the truth is young people in Hollywood are not supposed to be children, not in the work environment. The discipline is really important."

After weeks of missing call times and weeks of self-appointed "testing" of Disneyland racecar prototypes nearby on the lot, Paul sealed his fate with an outburst over the nickname the crew had given him because of his small stature: "Mouse." "I hated that nickname," he says. "One man above all others persisted in [using] this nickname, and that was Lee Travers, the head of casting, a very big, fat man. On this infamous Friday he walked up behind me after lunch, tapped me on the shoulder, and said, 'Hey, Mouse, how ya doin'?' Perfectly pleasant. Except I turned around and punched him in the stomach and said, 'Don't call me that, Fatso.' The problem was that hidden behind this massive man was Walt Disney. That's what did it."

Paul had gone much farther in front of the Big Boss than just smearing fake blood on himself like Dennis had. But even in the moment, Paul didn't realize the white wall phone in his home would ring that night, his mother would answer it, her face would drop, and she would hand the receiver to him. One of the adult staffers broke the news in the simplest terms: "Paul, we are sorry, but because of the discipline problems you are discharged." (Paul would go on to much greater stardom, first as Jeff Stone on *The Donna Reed Show* from 1958 to 1966, then as a chart-topping bubblegum pop star and a film actor, before becoming a child-star advocate.)

Petersen's frequent partners in crime, Mickey Rooney Jr. and

Tim Rooney—actor Mickey Rooney's sons—soon left as well. Their dismissal was thanks mostly to their antics with Paul, but the final straw apparently came when they found some paint cans backstage—to be used on one of the sets under construction—and mixed all the colors together to create an expensive and time-consuming mess for frazzled producers, who were growing more stressed by the day. Firings could come at any time for any reason now: There was even a kid who was rumored to have gotten axed just because his or her mom sat on the casting director's lap, though it's not clear who it was or if it was true. If all the firings weren't a shrewd strategic maneuver on the part of producers to keep the "good" kids in line, it indeed played that way: All of a sudden the remaining Mouseketeers (and, for the most part, their parents) were on their best behavior. They were hitting their marks and remembering their routines—at least the best they could. They weren't goofing around between takes or talking back to producers. They were donning claustrophobia-inducing animal costumes and dancing their hearts out without complaint. No one felt so comfortable and safe anymore.

The dismissals, the constant rehearsals, and the ever-more-anxious adults around them spelled out a message to the Mouseketeers as clear as M-I-C-K-E-Y: They had to perform. And now, with less than three months before the show premiered on television, they were summoned to a pressing publicity task—helping to make Walt Disney's greatest dream, his Disneyland theme park, come true with a perfect opening day.

The Mice sashayed down Disneyland's Main Street as the temperature sizzled at ninety degrees, thrilled to be at opening day of the brand-new Disneyland theme park. They'd endured months of rehearsals and shot dozens of episodes of their *Mickey Mouse Club* show, but not a minute had aired yet, so they reveled in the break from taping.

Chaos reigned around them: Traffic in heretofore rural Anaheim, California, backed up for two miles in every direction from Disneyland. And while park officials had prepared to handle the attraction's fifteen thousand-person capacity, nearly double that number showed up for opening day thanks to thousands of counterfeit invitations. Over a back fence, impish party crashers were sneaking in via ladder, paying $5 per person to the ladder's owner for the privilege. Trash cans overflowed. July 17, 1955, was memorable for all the wrong reasons—it would forever be referred to as "Black Sunday" around the Disney offices. But the kids couldn't have been happier to be making their first official appearance on the airwaves, to the 70 million viewers (that is, almost half the population of the United States at the time) watching Disneyland's opening on ABC. "There was no water in the water fountains, they were running out of food," Sharon remembers. "But for us it was fabulous. It was nothing but fun."

The little performers were still unknown to the world, which made this appearance, well, confusing. Not to the Mouseketeers themselves, who were more concerned with doing what they were told, but to the TV announcers trying to make sense of the festivities. "We were already filming, but we didn't know if the show was going to be a hit or not," Sharon remembers. "I don't think people knew who we were when we came down the street in the parade." Indeed, as they sashayed down Main Street behind crudely costumed characters (a gap-toothed Mickey and a Donald Duck costume with a human head), ABC parade announcer Art Linkletter, baffled by the "Mouseketeer" moniker, stumbled: "And here come all the little children, they're the...the...what?" Finally, he got it—almost: "They're the performing children who are going to be on the Disneyland *Mickey Mouse Club*."

Rounds and rounds of sweaty, nervous auditions and months of rehearsing and shooting had all added up to seven seconds of Linkletter fumbling their introduction. But the Mice marched on at the time, oblivious to how their grand entrance played on-air. "I was in the flurry, just as everyone else was," Lonnie says. "I was just smiling and making sure I did my stuff right because, particularly if you're a pro, you really care about that. So I always did. It's just the way I was." In fact, in the Mouseketeers' minds, being in the new park full of rides and games outshone the concept of appearing on camera: "What kid wouldn't enjoy something like that?" Sharon says. They'd even get their run of the park afterward, becoming enamored of the Mad Tea Party's teacups; the boys loved spinning them as fast as possible in hopes of making their fellow Mice sick.

"Most amusement parks in those days were more like carnivals, not very wholesome experiences," Cubby says. "But Disneyland was different, was like nothing we'd ever seen."

Their first real television performance came later in the broadcast when they danced at the Mickey Mouse Club Theater in Fantasyland. It was then that they finally got their proper introduction to the huge TV audience watching: "I guarantee you many a future star will be coming out of this group," ABC cohost Bob Cummings said on the air, more clear than Linkletter about who these kids were. Out they came to rush through a manic version of their "Talent Round-Up" song, most of them in fringed blue Western wear, galloping and jigging complete with prop horses, boots, and cowboy hats. The ears that would later become their most enduring trademark wouldn't show up until a minute and a half into the number on a select few tap-dancers. For the big finish, Lonnie recalls, "We did Roll Call. And this is significant, because it's the only time when all the kids who were on the show that year got to be in a Roll Call. Because, you know, only the Red Team got to do it on the TV show. But at Disneyland, all twenty-four of us got to say our names on television."

The Mouseketeers as we know them had arrived—but now it was time to get back to making a TV show. Their premiere date was less than three months away, and there was still a lot to be done. "The opening was a nice break from filming, and a preview of what our lives would be like," Cubby says. "The audience seemed excited, so we were excited about returning to work at the studio."

*   *   *

Viewers and Art Linkletter may not have been sure what they'd just seen, but that October, when the show officially debuted, there was no question. All the Mouseketeers' hard work paid off in an instant hit, enthralling ten million young viewers. Suddenly, they were a phenomenon. Publicity appearances inspired mob scenes wherever the Mice went. When they landed in Portland, Oregon, more than three thousand children and parents were waiting for them, even though their arrival had not been announced. Stops in Chicago and Dallas drew similar crowds. The Mouseketeers even got the ultimate affirmation of their fame when a rumor spread through elementary schools across America that they'd died in a bus accident, prompting Disney to print out postcards with their pictures to prove they were alive and well. Says Tommy, "I couldn't walk anywhere in the United States without being recognized. It was fun, but you had to keep your head, because you could start believing your publicity."

The show generated a whopping 7,500 letters per month, with fans expressing their admiration with a certain familiarity most Hollywood productions didn't engender. Sure, they requested the standard autographed photos, but they also casually asked to, say, borrow props or book themselves on the show. "Today I saw your program and I saw the dance some children did," one letter said. "It was a western dance. The children were riding play ponies. Halloween will soon be here. My mother is going to make a cowgirl suit for me so I wondered if you could send me one of those ponies." Another, addressed to Jimmie, said, "A girlfriend of mine and I would like to know if on Round-Up day in about four weeks we could be on your show. We would like to sing. Our ages are ten and eleven and we live in Lansing, Michigan." Even military men wrote in "because they had gone away from their family and would watch the show because we felt like a family," Sharon says. "Some people even sent rings and stuff that we'd have to send back."

Even jaded television critics, for the most part, couldn't deny the show's appeal. "There's never been anything like *Mickey Mouse* to hit television," entertainment industry paper *Variety* gushed. "It's the type of show that will appeal to adults," *Billboard* said, "not those with a juvenile mind, but those who enjoy children—enjoy watching them at play, at work, and growing up." The *Los Angeles Times*, in one of the understatements of the century, predicted, "You can be sure the kids will have a new theme song to whistle and sing for months to come." Only the *New York Times* begged to differ, saying the premiere "bordered on disastrous" and was "only irritatingly cute and contrived and bereft of any semblance of the justly famous Disney touch." Worse, critic Jack Gould called the Mouseketeers "a group of youngsters evidently... borrowed from the children's amateur hours around the country." (Clearly Gould didn't realize that was the *point*.) But kids and moms sided with *Variety* and *Billboard*, and that was all that mattered.

By February 1956 *The Mickey Mouse Club* reached more total viewers than any other daytime program—more than three times the viewers of *Pinky Lee,* more than twice the audience of *Howdy Doody.* It was even nominated for an Emmy. Producers, however, chose not to go out of their way to inform their charges of their growing popularity. The great ratings and gangbuster merchandise sales remained a topic of adult conversation only. "They said, 'We're doing okay, just keep working, just keep dancing,'" Tommy says. Many of the Mousekemoms and -dads were trying to keep their little stars involved with their pre–Mouse Club friends and activities, emphasizing some sense of normal childhood in contrast to the mob scenes the kids occasionally encountered at autograph sessions or public performances. "My parents made sure I didn't neglect being just a kid," Cubby says. "I played Little League baseball. I'd go across the street to the park and do stuff with my friends. I still kept my friendships with the neighborhood boys."

Hints as to their level of stardom did sometimes sneak through, however, even when the Mice were trying to live their normal lives: "When I would get through shooting and come home," Sharon recalls, "neighborhood kids would be sitting on the fence wanting to know what we did that day. So I knew we were popular."

Life overall felt pretty regular for the Mouseketeers once they settled into their new roles as preteen idols. They went to class. They respected their elders. They ate lunch in the commissary and hung out with their friends. But their everyday lives did differ in one key way: They happened in the shadow of Walt Disney. And that made more difference than the Mice could realize at the time.

Chapter Five

Life in Disney's World

Mr. Walt Disney was strolling along his studio lot's landscape full of giant peachy-pink boxes that served as soundstages—dark hair slicked back, pipe dangling below his tidy mustache, a suited executive by his side. For him, it was like so many typically flawless Southern California days there in his Burbank kingdom, but when he noticed a Mouseketeer happening by, he sprinkled a bit of his famous magic on the kid with one simple action. He greeted his prized little corporate symbol—by *name*. Casually, brightly, as if they were pals, as if they chatted every day. Now, a total of thirty-nine Mouseketeers wore those ears during *The Mickey Mouse Club*'s three years of production, so this individualized greeting was quite something.

At least three separate Mice have claimed this story as their own, each adding his or her own details. Lonnie Burr says he immediately scampered away, his smile as bright as his blond hair in the sun, ready to brag to anyone who'd listen: Mr. Disney knew his name! Until the realization struck a few seconds later: The true reason for the big boss's easy recognition? The trademark Mouseketeer sweater, name emblazoned across the chest in letters bigger than the top row of an eyesight-test chart. In Tommy Cole's recounting, he ran over to the movie theater on the lot where the parents spent most of their time to tell Mom the good news: "I was really sort of stoked until she looked down at me and said, 'What are you wearing?'" In second-season Mouse Sherry Alberoni's version, Mom hovered right next to her, ready to set her pigtailed darling straight. Sherry looked up at her, wide-eyed with awe, gushing, "Mommy, Mommy, he knows my name!" Mom, ever the sensible June Cleaver character, chuckled. "Honey," she whispered, "your shirt."

Lonnie, for one, goes out of his way to insist that the charming anecdote is all his and has been pilfered by his costars over years of retelling charming anecdotes; and it is, in fact, quite possible that it happened to all three of them on separate occasions. Let's just say, for the sake of moving past it, that this story has made a cozy home for itself in the collective Mousekememory. Which Mouse it happened to is, in fact, beside the point: What's more telling is how much it meant to the Mouseketeers to be recognized by the father figure of the entertainment empire of which they were a small part.

Being part of the Disney family meant the world to the young stars, many of whom had tried out for the show and signed on without a second thought because it meant joining the company that brought the world *Sleeping Beauty, Bambi,* Mickey Mouse, and, now, Disneyland. Because of that, just spending every day on the studio lot where the magic happened granted the Mouseketeers their share of memorable moments. After all, most kids in America would've been thrilled just to see Walt Disney in person, regardless of whether he knew their names. And it was the most magical details of the Mouseketeers' everyday lives during their *Mickey Mouse Club* days that stayed with them: the time they spent learning in the on-set schoolhouse trailer, the run-ins with famous fellow Disney stars at lunch, the bonding with their costars during publicity tours—and, of course, the sight of Walt Disney himself watching from the back of the soundstage as they rehearsed. Life in Walt Disney's considerable shadow—and in service to the Disney Studios family—definitely had its sunny side. Although, as with belonging to any family, it had its darker side, too—adult tensions that trickled down to the Mouseketeers, strict discipline, and, in keeping with the Disney ethos, loads of hard work.

Walt sightings played a key part in the Mouseketeers' lives—since the mogul meant so much to *them*, even though they were but a fraction of his business. Walt's level of contribution to *The Mickey Mouse Club* as a whole, however, would prove a continued subject for debate. During *The Mickey Mouse Club* years, Walt was opening Disneyland, venturing into live-action films, and maintaining some presence in the animated world in addition to growing his television empire. Legend seems to have exaggerated his role in the

Club slightly—probably because most of the Mice knew who he was, knew he'd handpicked Annette, and felt his implied presence in their everyday lives.

Annette swears in her autobiography that she saw him constantly—and given that she was by far his favorite, perhaps she *did* see him more than others did. "He made sure that we were having fun," she writes. "There wasn't a day when he didn't drop by the set to see how things were going, to ask us if we needed anything, to simply say hello." But others have wondered how much he really liked kids, and Lonnie directly disputes Annette's rendering: "It's over fifty years ago, and some Mouseketeers started building up these myths. Walt was around all the time? Walt was around a lot because that's where he worked, but he was on our sets very rarely. Obviously we shot a couple of things with Walt in them, so he's going to be there. But just occasionally." Sharon says he *was* around, but he didn't always make his presence well-known: "He was very quiet and soft-spoken," she says, "and he would sit in the back of the soundstage and be in his little paint pants and shirt because he had been in the paint department mixing paint with the guys. So he *was* involved." How often and for how long, however, is apparently subject to Mouskememory.

Regardless of whether Walt Disney was constantly around the Mouseketeers, he did go out of his way to make them feel a part of the Disney family. "Walt would come down on birthday days, and we'd stop and have cake and ice cream," Cubby says. "Walt Disney coming down with a sheet cake? And I get to stand next to him and he's singing 'Happy Birthday' to me? This was great!" Walt also, according to some Mice, was fiercely protective of their young sensibilities. Many Mouseketeers report that the least hint of anything other than G-rated behavior on the set could get a staffer dismissed. "Walt Disney wouldn't allow the people on set to swear around us," Sharon maintains. Annette even adds, "If Walt Disney learned that anyone—even an adult—had uttered so much as a 'damn,' you could be sure you wouldn't see him on the set the next day." However, it should be noted, some oft-quoted anecdotes negate this: Director Dik Darley was once greeted on set by a sign that read DIK IS A PRK. And many say Roy Williams was always good for a bit of a foul-mouthed remark or a somewhat naughty story. But according to Tommy no one got offended. "He was that kind of fun, fun character."

And the times when Walt Disney was around, he was nothing but supportive of his young charges, who still got nervous every time they saw him. One of his nerve-wracking appearances on set even ended up making for a clever publicity gambit. Tommy had been using his smooth speaking voice to lend a kiddie-level gravitas to the intros and outros for the newsreel segments, for which he'd sometimes don thematic costumes and props—a dark suit and hat for an FBI report, for instance. During the taping for one segment, however, he continued to flub his lines—because he saw Walt Disney, the man who could make or break him, hovering right next to the camera, smack in the middle of his eye-line. "I was doing all the ins and outs with a teleprompter," Tommy recalls.

"And sometimes it was pretty long dialogue with no cuts; it's just straight into the camera, 'Hi, I'm Tommy Cole, this is this and that,' and, 'We're meeting with so-and-so today.' It's a long little diatribe."

No matter what he did, he couldn't get through the lengthy chunk of dialogue—producers shot it straight through, so he had to nail it without a glitch before they could move on. "Hi, I'm Tommy Cole," he said, before choking for the dozenth time.

At last, Tommy called an assistant director over and whispered a rather bold request: "Could you ask Mr. Disney to move over to the left, just a little bit? 'Cause he's making me nervous."

Tommy's well-trained singer's diaphragm sucked in and froze as the assistant director walked over to Disney through the silent, scattered crowd of crew members and producers, who were growing increasingly annoyed by having to stay there until the segment wrapped. When the AD whispered Tommy's request into Mr. Disney's ear, the response came: one serious nod, and a few steps to the left, out of sight.

It had turned out just fine, much to Tommy's relief. However, the studio publicity agents lurking in the back of the soundstage saw the potential in the incident. Figuring all press was good press, they tipped off the entertainment trade papers. The next day's headline, as Cole remembers it, may have overplayed the drama a smidge: MOUSEKETEER THROWS WALT DISNEY OFF THE SET. Tommy didn't mind, as long as he knew the true story: that Disney had been nothing but understanding. "Luckily Walt had a sense of humor," he says, "and I didn't get fired."

As sympathetic as Disney could be, no one disputes that Walt demanded a lot from his young stars. High expectations, clear rules, regimented days, and overwhelming work schedules were a way of life on the *Mickey Mouse Club* set. There was, in fact, an actual contract clause to "conduct yourself in a Disney-like manner," as Sharon describes it. "People have asked me, 'Are you the way you are because of Walt Disney, or did Walt Disney pick you because of the way you are?'" she says. "I think it's a combination of both. I think the Disney Studio had the charm of knowing what to do."

The producers and crew taught the kids to respect their elders, but also to see them as family: The Mice called all of the adults on set "Aunt" and "Uncle," as in "Uncle Makeup" for the makeup artist and "Aunt Hairdresser" for the hair stylist. They remained too in awe of Walt to address him on such a familiar level, however, even though the rest of the country knew him as Uncle Walt, host of *Disneyland*: "He wanted us to call him Uncle Walt," Sharon says. "We couldn't. No, in those days you respected your elders and it was Mr. Disney."

Most of the Mice wouldn't dare act up against the authority figures on set. Several former Mice remain convinced that their strongest skill was neither singing, nor dancing, nor acting, but simply behaving themselves. "They taught us," Bobby says. "Don't touch the props. Find out where the main light is, and don't cast a shadow on your fellow Mouseketeers. Be prepared. If you need to know your lines, go home and learn them."

Irresponsible behavior had monetary consequences as well: Those precious Mouse ears, for instance, were crucial to filming, and to show up without ears was to not show up at all. If a Mouse lost them, he or she had to pay for a new pair. Annette and Bobby counted themselves among the unlucky Mice who had their paychecks docked for a new beanie, which instantly instilled a commitment among their costars to never let their own ears out of their sight even for a second. "We were not allowed to take them off the studio lot," Mary says. "And if we lost one, it was fifty dollars. When Bobby lost his, he told me that—I didn't know that until he told me. So I really didn't want to lose my ears after that."

Learning lines and mastering studies took precedence over goofing off. "If you looked at the schedule, I'd say it could be considered grueling for a child," Mary says. "I had a carpool, so I got up really early and got home pretty late." Structure and authority figures also abounded around the production of *The Mickey Mouse Club*. With every kid having a guardian on the lot, the little stars knew a frustrated producer or director need do nothing more than walk a few steps to get them in trouble at home. The set was also crawling with producers, directors, cameramen, choreographers, and other crew members who numbered far more than the twenty-four Mouseketeers—the ratio of adults to children was almost ten to one. "If you're a kid in showbiz, the thing you learn is you are supported and surrounded by great adults," Mary says. "In a way it sets you up differently, to see the world differently than if you were just in regular school."

One of the Mouseketeers' biggest adult influences was their strict—though beloved—teacher, Mrs. Seaman. She had to keep military-precise order just to get her job done according to the law. She was, for instance, required to ensure that each of the twenty-four Mice got three hours of school per day, and the increments had to be at least twenty minutes long to count toward the total. That one obligation, in itself, represented a massive organizational job. "The teacher always fought for at least a half an hour so you could focus on what you were doing," Lonnie says. "It didn't always work out, and she was always hassled [by producers] about it. It's very difficult to be writing an essay on political science and then to have somebody say, 'Come on to the set.'"

The students would enter Mrs. Seaman's trailer—painted red like a schoolhouse—in groups of no more than ten, the maximum permitted by law, and sit in the two rows of desks down each side of the tiny space. The groups mixed ages and levels, with Mrs. Seaman ready to teach anything from first through twelfth grade, as well as subject matter, veering from Spanish to algebra as necessary, as quickly as production schedules demanded. Mrs. Seaman was, by most accounts, a tough, but fair, grader. They dreaded some of her lessons—literature and physiology could be a drag—but the kids loved a lot of their assignments, such as making posters about classical musicians. And they reveled in their Spanish lessons, for the most part because they got to pick alternate names: Kids would call Sharon "Susita" and Bobby "Roberto" even later during rehearsals and taping. "To this day I call Bobby 'Roberto,' and there's no Spanish name for Sharon so he made it up and called me 'Susita,'" Sharon says. "So I can come home and I'll have a message on the machine saying, *'Hola Susita!'* And I know that's my friend Roberto."

Most important of all, Mrs. Seaman pulled off the tough trick of giving the Mice a high-quality school experience despite the intense demands on their time. "It was all very concentrated," Tommy says. "There was no play, and we got enough exercise doing the dances. So it was straight work. But we really had a very good education." Bobby agrees: "I went back [to public school] my senior year in high school and graduated in the upper two percent of my class because of what I learned on set." Sharon adds, "You'd think only going three hours a day we'd be way behind, but we were so far ahead, because our own personal questions got answered all the time."

Staying on top of their schooling requirements was even more important for the Mouseketeers than for regular kids, as the state was constantly checking up on child stars. During the summer they could work eight hours a day, with an hour lunch break and no school. But during the school year, officials would check their progress with court appearances every six months, quizzing the kids about their studies and their feelings about work. The court asked pointed questions about everything from bed-wetting to eating habits. "Because I had never been a very good eater," Annette writes, "these periodic examinations worried Mom to no end, but I always passed." Adds Bobby, "They even checked our fingernails to make sure we weren't too nervous."

Though the Mouseketeers worked hard to answer to producers, their teacher, and state officials alike, they also enjoyed the perks of growing up on the studio lot. "I used to like to explore around the studio," John Lee Johann says. "I liked to see the stars and go to the different soundstages. It's amazing what you can get away with." Going to lunch at the right time meant bumping cafeteria trays with high-wattage Disney stars such as Davy Crockett himself, Fess Parker; Buddy Ebsen (who played Crockett sidekick Georgie Russell); or *Zorro's* Guy Williams. "Ooooh, that was a thrill, going to the cafeteria," Mary says, "because the cafeteria in the studio was the place everybody ate who was filming anything at Disney. So Fess Parker and Buddy Ebsen were right next to me with their little trays, getting food, just like us, because it was all cafeteria-style."

Many of the boys would spend their lunchtimes playing Ping-Pong in the penthouse of the main building on the lot, holding their own against the adults—the three on-campus tables were open to the entire Disney Productions staff. "I didn't eat much because I was always playing Ping-Pong," Tommy remembers. "They didn't want me in the tournaments because I'd always win." Other Mice would wander off to the animation building where the all-female staff—because they had hands delicate enough for the detailed work—inked and painted the cels that would become Mickey, Goofy, and the gang in cartoon movies. "The crazy thing is, somebody offered me one," Mary says, "and I was too silly to accept it. I just thought, 'We have to go back to rehearsal now.'"

The Mice were, in reality, often shielded from the harshest realities of working for Disney, which, like any successful business, made its share of cold, corporate-minded decisions. "There was a certain amount of pressure, but it was more on the adults, to get this done right," Cubby says. "They were coordinating it with the opening of Disneyland that year and their new association with ABC television, so it was a big deal." But the kids occasionally caught a glimpse of what was really going on, namely when they had to say good-bye to several of the adult staffers they loved.

The first time the Mice felt the sting of the grownups' behind-the-scenes politics was near the end of the first season, when they arrived on set one morning in early 1956 to find that their suave director, Dik Darley, had vanished. The Mouseketeers loved Darley. Sharon nursed a huge crush on him; Lonnie adored him. "He reminded me of a young Johnny Carson," Lonnie says. "He always dressed [up]. He always wore a suit and tie on the set and he was very cool and polite, he was very together and knew what he was doing." The Mice simply couldn't believe the man with the gentle demeanor and the closet full of sharp suits, with whom they'd shared every stressful day for the past nine months, had disappeared on them without warning.

Now they faced new director Sidney Miller, a dark, sinewy, brash former actor who had, of late, been working with Donald O'Connor on *The Colgate Comedy Hour* and on O'Connor's own show. Miller had now come to make *The Mickey Mouse Club* slicker and cooler, with a directive from Disney to capitalize on and hone the show's burgeoning hit status, to target the growing teenage audience instead of just young preteens.

Miller certainly succeeded in eliciting an instant strong reaction from the Mice themselves. Some loved his goofy approach, directing as if he were doing a bumbling physical comedy bit *about* being the director of a kids' show. He stuck cigarettes up his nose to make the kids laugh. When Karen needed an endless thirty-two takes to get through a vitamin commercial message without giggling, he fell down on the floor mock-sobbing, begging her theatrically to please get it right. It just made her giggle more: "He was real funny like that. He was sometimes gruff, but he always came around to make up."

But he was also more demanding than Darley. Tommy says Miller once berated him to the point of real tears in front of his fellow Mouseketeers for not knowing the words to a song. Third-season Mouseketeer Don Agrati says he once chased a kid around with a burning cigarette, muttering, "Come here, you little brat...." Miller would usually apologize after such incidents, and certainly never physically harmed anyone, but nonetheless, he often seemed to forget he was trying to coax shining performances out of children—many of whom didn't get his sense of humor—rather than trying to make adults laugh.

"Sid shouldn't have been dealing with kids," Lonnie says. "I was a professional and cared a great deal about what I was doing, I didn't make many mistakes, and his attitude was still unpleasant." Lonnie had a slew of run-ins with the new director, including one of his most embarrassing moments as a Mouseketeer. "We did a Tyrolean number, and they made us wear these obscene shorts and suspenders with crap all over them and hats with feathers in them," he remembers. "I was in the front with Sharon, dancing. And near the beginning of the segment, my pants ripped from below the zipper all the way up to my waistband. And my underpants are showing! The putz who was the director then [Miller], I didn't get along with him. And he didn't even notice! So I went after the shot to tell him, and he said, 'Don't bother me, kid.' But I finally got to him and said, 'My pants were ripped. You're going to see underpants.' And he acted like I'd done it on purpose to ruin the show, so I said, 'Hey, I didn't make the costume.' They reshot it [eventually], but it was embarrassing for me."

Many wondered if Miller had, in fact, even wanted the job. "He used to bang his head on the floor," Cubby recalls, demonstrating the frustrated director's infuriated motions and grunts. "Of course we didn't know then that it was five o'clock and he wanted to go home. You know, 'Let's get the hell out of here.'"

What the Mouseketeers also didn't know was that the unexpected strife on the set of *The Mickey Mouse Club* reflected a larger anxiety spreading throughout Walt Disney Studios. Their beloved Mr. Disney had developed an unfortunate firing habit. The entire Disney staff had, in fact, taken on a nervous twitch over the previous few years that was nearing nervous-breakdown levels for some. His employees lived in fear, and word of Walt's fickle employment practices was spreading to the rest of Hollywood. Director Richard Fleischer arrived on the lot to make *20,000 Leagues Under the Sea* having heard but written off the stories as hearsay—until he talked to his new boss about them. "You know, every once in a while I just fire everybody," Walt admitted when Fleischer brought the rumors up. "Then I hire them back in a couple of weeks. That way they don't get complacent. It keeps them on their toes."

It worked—one employee at the time noted that Disney's employees "would fervently agree even if he said two plus two was twenty-two." And the firings continued, trickling down to *The Mickey Mouse Club*. "Check on everybody in the Mouseketeer group who has been carried over," Walt directed his producers. "I believe that outside of the nine [Red Team] Mouseketeers, Jimmy [sic] Dodd and Roy Williams, we should start from scratch....Let's make a thorough check on the setup of the Mouseketeers and see that we are not carrying people who are not needed."

Change was in store. First came Darley's exit. Next went Bob Amsberry, the amiable character actor and sometime lyricist who handled the most thankless of on-air responsibilities, using his radio-honed voice characterization skills to play adult supporting roles to the kid stars. Deemed superfluous to the show by the end of the first season, he was officially fired in September 1956. Just two months later he died in a car accident back home in Portland, at age twenty-nine, when his sports car veered off the highway and into a light pole. Because of the unfortunate timing, most of the Mice thought his tenure had ended with his death, rather than a dismissal. "He was very funny," Tommy recalls. "He always played our characters, he wore a big mustache or beard, just a real character player. It's too bad he couldn't have been with the show the whole time. He was a fun character."

Hal Adelquist—a twenty-three-year Disney veteran whom Walt had once upon a time handpicked to help Bill Walsh conceive the show—ran into even more trouble with the big boss. Adelquist handled carrying out the intricacies of everyone else's ideas—overseeing casting, finding guest stars, working with the costumer to make those famous ears, making every correction Walt demanded whenever he happened to turn his perfectionist eye toward *The Mickey Mouse Club*. For instance, Adelquist later explained to the *New York Times*, "For some reason Walt didn't like ventriloquist acts. So I had to watch out for that."

By the end of the first season, the frustration and exhaustion were getting to him even more than the rest of the adult staffers, and for good reason—he was the one trying to coordinate all of them. Adelquist was soon demoted to doing nothing but finding Talent Round-Up Day winners for the second season during a ten-city tour with Jimmie. Adelquist left the studio shortly thereafter, then begged Walt to give him another chance, even writing to him, "I'm not particular about the kind of work involved." But Walt declined. To the kids, Uncle Hal had simply gone away, and no explanation was ever given. "He was real hands-on," Bobby says. "He was just everybody's friend. But once he was gone, we never heard what happened to him after that."

Just because the Mice didn't know what was going on behind the scenes with the adults on set, however, didn't mean they were exempt from contributing to Disney's overall bottom line. Being part of the Disney family also meant earning their keep by participating in publicity and marketing. Lots of it.

For example, it was in the name of corporate synergy that Doreen Tracey found herself frozen high up on a platform at Disneyland, looking down at the crowd below, paralyzed by her fear. The Mice had been dispatched to lure crowds to the amusement park by performing a Mickey Mouse Club Circus on weekends, and Doreen hadn't flinched at the suggestion that she should do an aerial act—after all, her first showbiz job had been as the ringleader of an all-girls circus. She had proved herself perfect for the Disneyland job when the circus opened on November 24, 1955; her act was a highlight of the seventy-five-minute show. She delighted in the audience's awed reaction, just like she always did, natural performer that she was.

Then, a few weeks in, she forgot her trainer's crucial instruction to not look down. When she did, she froze there, up on the platform, just the tiny plank of wood supporting her high above the crowd. She couldn't move until the crew brought her a ladder.

Sharon, on the other hand, had an easier time doing the "web" (basically a rope hanging from the ceiling on which she and costar Bonnie Lynn Fields would twirl and flip while wearing glowy, fluorescent costumes in the dark). She loved it so much it was hard to get her to stop practicing: "When we were rehearsing at the studio, they said, 'Okay, let's see if any of you can get up there,'" she recalls. "I went *sssshhp*, up the rope until my mother came in—it was time for us to go to lunch—and said, 'Sharon, what are you doing, get down from there!' That was one of my favorite moments."

"All the girls were dressed like Tinkerbell," Mary recalls. "We were on these high poles, and we'd pose ourselves in different positions against them. There was a trampoline, there was a trapeze. It was pretty dangerous, but it was fun."

As much fun as the circus was for the Mice, the endeavor ultimately became an early reminder that fun was not the primary goal here. And, more surprisingly, that there were limits to the Disney marketing machine's powers: The company axed the circus after little more than a month when attendance simply didn't meet expectations—enthusiastic though many *Mickey Mouse Club* fans were, they either couldn't or didn't make the trek to Southern California to see their heroes fly through the air with the greatest of ease.

Other publicity gambits proved both fun and fruitful, as when the Mouseketeers embarked on a cross-country publicity tour between the first and second seasons, bringing their act to their fans instead of expecting fans to come to them. They found thousands of admirers gathered to greet them, get their autographs, and see them perform at every tour stop. But the best moments for the Mice came aboard two private railroad cars known as the Disney Express.

The kids slept in the upper berths, their parents in the lower. During the day, as the train roared across the country, the two youngest Mice, Cubby and Karen, played with whatever treat Cubby's mom had gifted them with that day—a tiny plastic number or spelling game, a coloring book. The older kids would cue up a portable record player and dance in whatever space they could find. "We went to the observation car and pushed all the chairs and tables aside," Sharon says. "So, if you can believe this, while the train is going along, we're playing music and dancing." No stage choreography for a few blissful hours.

At night, Annette's father, Joe Funicello, would mix drinks in the back of the train for the parents as well as Roy and Jimmie, who enjoyed the occasional martini—with Christian moderation. The kids would sneak into Doreen's berth for a slumber party of sorts, a dream come true for young Cubby, who was in love with all the teenage girls: Doreen, Annette, and Darlene. "It was fun to be with a bunch of other kids, older kids," Cubby says.

Sometimes Roy would even slip a tiny shot of whatever was in his flask into a few of the older kids' sodas during the cross-country trips, Doreen says. "When we would go out and do road shows, he thought it was great fun to give us a shot in our Cokes," she says. "Not all of them, because some of them were very proper young boys and girls like Bobby. Bobby was always like that—'Let's play by the rules.' But you know, you have to have someone like that to have balance, especially with me and a few of the others around."

Aboard that train, without enough room to rehearse numbers—and with *The Mickey Mouse Club*'s filming on a summer hiatus anyway—the Mice got to act like kids for a while, whether that meant playing games or listening to pop music or sneaking their first tastes of rebellion. "It was fun," Karen says. "I never considered it work. I used to get tired sometimes, but I really didn't think about it. I just did it."

When they got to wherever they were going, though, they got back to business, serious professionals ready to perform again, and again, and again, for their waiting fans. The national, forty-city tour marked the first time many of the Mice understood just how popular they'd become. "When I think we really realized the show was a hit was when we went on that train trip to Chicago from L.A.," Tommy says. "We did stops at different places, and all these people kept showing up. And we're going, 'Wow, we must really have a lot of PR on this.' We were mobbed. They'd come out by the throngs and just be cheering for us."

Karen, in particular, was at first baffled by the idea that she could be the least bit famous. Once when a guy on the street asked for her autograph, "I had no idea why," she says. "It just didn't register for me when I was a little kid." The man, as a joke, suggested she get a stamp of her name since she would, without a doubt, be signing many autographs; she took his suggestion literally, having her mother get her a stamp of her name—but the first girl she used it on complained that a real signature was the whole point. "I just didn't understand the significance of having me write my name," Karen says.

One particular stop on the tour, however, brought them even closer to a group of local fans. On an icy weekday on the road in New England, Jimmie, determined to watch the five p.m. airing of that day's episode, told the bus driver to stop at the next house they saw with bicycles in front of it. "That way we know they have kids," he said, "and if they have kids, they have to be watching the show."

They found a promising-looking place, and Jimmie rang the bell. "I have a busload of Mouseketeers here who would like to stop in and see the show," he told the couple who answered. "Would it be okay?"

The sarcastic response: "Sure, *sure*, you have Mouseketeers!"

Unperturbed, Jimmie beckoned his charges to come inside. The Mice, in full uniform, flooded the strangers' living room. The parents and their five children, once recovered from the shock, called all their neighbors to come by and see their famous guests; then they served the little stars a delicious dinner.

Even when the Mice returned to their own Southern California homes from the cross-country tour, publicity, public appearances, parades, charity dinners, and tours took up almost all of their waking time not devoted to the show. The memos detailing scheduled personal appearances came fast and relentlessly. A typical weekend might include a Friday evening stop at a department store and three more throughout the day on Saturday. The Mice performed at some places, signed autographs at others. Cars would pick the Mouseketeers up in the morning and take them to their scheduled locations. "Please wear a top coat," their instruction memos would remind them, "so that you will not easily be identifiable on the street."

It was hard to believe, with crowds clamoring for just a glimpse of the Mouseketeers, but there was some serious competition for the hearts of their very own viewership—from a threat tucked way out in the dusty Southern California wilderness at a place called the Triple R Ranch. A flood of mail would deluge *The Mickey Mouse Club* addressed not to Annette or Lonnie or Bobby or Sharon, but to none other than two guys named Spin and Marty. It would drown out the fan bases of nearly all the Mice in its wake—and even make Mouse ears seem, suddenly, just a little...uncool.

Chapter Six

Spin and Marty

The Adventures of Two *Mickey Mouse Club* Heartthrobs

Not everyone on *The Mickey Mouse Club* was a Mouseketeer, but a few of those kid actors on the *other* parts of the show—the ones populating the serial segments—would do what seemed impossible at the moment: They would become at least as famous as the Mouseketeers, the most envied kids in America.

In fact, when fourteen-year-old actor Tim Considine first encountered the Mouseketeers at Disney Studios one late summer day, he was more perplexed than impressed. "I remember seeing these kids with names on their shirts," he remembers. "And I thought, 'Isn't that peculiar. What is that about?'" So after eating lunch in the commissary, he followed the kids at an undetectable distance until they returned to their home base, Sound Stage 1. When he peeked in and saw them singing and dancing, he thought, *Shoot, I'm glad I don't have to do that!* He had to admit, though, he was a little envious that they all got to hang around with the pretty dark-haired girl whose name, it seemed from her sweater, was Annette. So *these* were the Mouseketeers. "That was the first time I ever had any consciousness of *The Mickey Mouse Club*," Tim says. "And then gradually it became known to me that we were a part of that somehow."

The fact was, he happened to play Spin in *The Adventures of Spin and Marty*, the story of a poor, scrappy type who takes on a rich, snotty newcomer named Marty at the Triple R Ranch boys' summer camp. He'd been shooting the serial with his buddy David Stollery as his costar, and it was, as it turned out, running as a segment of *The Mickey Mouse Club*, even though the boys preferred to think of it as its own, separate work. "We were part of *The Mickey Mouse Club*, but we were also independent," Tim says. "And that was kind of fun for me, because I have *quite* an independent streak."

While other serials would run as part of the show both before (*What I Want to Be*) and after (*Corky and White Shadow, The Hardy Boys' Mystery of the Applegate Treasure*), none would have the same impact as *Spin and Marty*, with its horse ranch fantasy-camp setting and its heroes, who radiated boyish charm and friendly chemistry through its twenty-five short (ten-minute) installments. Viewers loved it so much, it would spawn two sequels in the show's second and third seasons, make genuine heartthrobs of its two stars, and become so well known that many fans thought it was its very own show.

For viewers, the famous pairing started on the November 7, 1955, episode, just a month into *The Mickey Mouse Club*'s first season, with Martin Markham pouting in the backseat of a shiny black livery cab, his fedora, houndstooth suit, and bowtie just so. He was running late, having stopped off to buy more summer-camp-appropriate clothing, T-shirt-type stuff he'd never owned before. "I didn't want to come to any old boys' ranch in the first place," he whined to his butler, Perkins, who was sitting up front in the passenger seat next to the driver.

"The Triple R isn't just any old boys' ranch, Master Markham," Perkins assured him in a British accent. "And for a boy with no experience with such places and no acquaintanceship with other lads, well, it seems to me that it would be rather a good thing for you."

But just as they crossed the dirt-road entrance to the dusty cluster of stables and bunks that would serve as the wealthy chap's improbable home for the summer, a plaid-shirted, blue-jeaned Spin Evans, riding a burro, ambled out in front of the Cadillac. The driver hit the brakes, sending Martin tumbling to the floor of the car. When Martin pulled himself up, hat askew, to look out the car window to see what had gotten in his way, history happened: Spin and Marty were clashing for the first of many memorable times.

That's how things looked in black-and-white to the millions of kids who'd wish they could spend *their* summers at the Triple R ranch, riding horses, warming up to cranky Marty and winning over all-star Spin. But they'd have to settle for just watching on their TVs as the boys taunted each other, mastered horseback riding, boxed to solve their disputes, and sang yet another catchy song churned out by the Disney tune factory. That was the round-the-campfire ditty "The Triple R Song," written by former National Park Ranger and *Spin and Marty* costar Stan Jones. The familiar refrain: *"Way out there on the Triple R, yippee-yay-ay, yippee-yo."*

But in the full color of real life, the freckle-faced Tim Considine and the towheaded David Stollery met a few years before shooting to stardom as Spin and Marty. And like their characters, the boys who played Spin and Marty came to their careers from opposite directions.

David was groomed from birth to be a stage kid. "My mother's the one who got me into the business," David explains. "I've had a job since I was six. So that's why I keep working, because that's what I know how to do. If you start when you're six, you learn how to show up and be quiet and take direction." That discipline landed David a small part in *A Connecticut Yankee in King Arthur's Court* at six years old and the lead in a 1953 Broadway revival of *On Borrowed Time*—a large, dramatic part for someone so young that won him a "child actor of the year" award. "I had done a lot of TV, a lot of film, and a lot of serious, live theater," David says. "So [*Spin and Marty*] was just another deal. I had never done a series before, and Tim and I and everyone else involved had no idea the impact this would have on American culture."

Tim, on the other hand, grew up among Hollywood's elite—with neither he, nor his parents, ever caring whether he got into acting. Tim's family was as interwoven with the burgeoning movie industry as they could be: His father, John W. Considine Jr., produced a slew of the earliest Hollywood films, including *Boys Town* and *Puttin' on the Ritz*. His mom, Carmen Pantages, came from the family that owned the Los Angeles theater chain bearing their name. Tim was the kind of kid who'd end up with a copy of *The Son of the Sheik* script signed by Rudolph Valentino and shrug it off, not even remembering how exactly he'd gotten it. As such, he had what David calls "a confidence bordering on arrogance that was rather charming." Tim also had the luxury of calling his acting career quits at any time—and he did so often. "Unlike most child actors, I was *permitted* by my parents to act," he says. "They did not *encourage* it at all. My father produced forty-three movies. What the hell did he care whether I was ever in a movie? They were never impressed with it, and that was to my great advantage. That was what I had that virtually no one else had."

David and Tim's first off-screen meeting, however, showed that from the start they were a duo of kindred spirits that was meant to be, a mini Butch and Sundance waiting to happen. They first noticed each other a few years before *Spin and Marty* as they traversed the same acting circuits. "We were on an audition together, and I had a model car in my hand," Tim recalls. "The rest of the child actors were kind of manic and going at it, and that intimidated me. So I just held on to my little car. And I don't know that David was intimidated too, but he *was* quiet like me. Finally, though, he walked around the perimeter and came to me and admired my car." An immediate bond formed. A few years later, the two cool, composed boys gravitated toward each other again when they worked with a cast full of youthful stars on the 1954 boarding-school drama *Her Twelve Men.* "We were mates," Tim says. "We used to play with those cars together. And little toy soldiers. He had little toy soldiers, and I loved that, too."

Their destinies would become intertwined from then on.

Both of their paths to the Triple R began with Tim's first "retirement" at the age of just fourteen. Having dabbled in films from Red Skelton's *The Champ* to Oscar-nominee *Executive Suite,* he'd appeared in an NBC pilot for a TV series based on the popular radio show *The Great Gildersleeve,* about a womanizer who took care of his orphaned niece and nephew (whom Tim played).

What could've been a breakout role for the young actor, however, crumbled into a notorious disaster when director Frank Tashlin spent all of his time focusing on the young opera singer Mary Costa—who, though cast in a minor role, happened to be Tashlin's wife. The pilot project soon turned into *The Mary Costa Show,* which the network didn't pick up, so executives ordered a brand-new *Gildersleeve* be shot instead. "The second pilot, I didn't get along with the director very much, and I had kind of a scene with him," Tim recalls. "He yelled at my stand-in for something I had done, and reduced this poor kid to tears. I lost it. It was the first time, really, that I hadn't enjoyed what I was doing. So I said, 'I'm not going to do that anymore.' NBC was a little upset because they sold the pilot and then I wasn't going to be in it. They threatened me, 'You'll never work again!' I was fourteen years old, what the hell did I care?"

Tim figured he was done with Hollywood—until a few months later when his agent told him Disney was looking for young male actors. "Well, Disney was a magic word," he says. "So only because of that, I went to read for the part. *Disneyland* was on then, and I thought anything with Disney was fantastic." Tim, however, at first auditioned for the part of rich-kid Marty, shooting a screen test for the scene in which Marty comes face-to-terrified-face with a horse named Skyrocket for the first time. He read for the part because it was a solo lead at the time—the series was based on a book called *Marty Markham*.

The audition went by in a blur for the cocky teenager, who was more enamored of the fact that trying out at Disney Studios meant playing baseball all day long with the other potential Martys. "There was this huge grass field with a baseball diamond on it," Tim remembers. "It was very cool." Tim pitched for part of the game, during which he noticed a stocky, balding guy crouching just behind the batter, a cigar hanging out the side of his mouth. He later found out that guy calling the game from home plate was none other than *Mickey Mouse Club* executive producer Bill Walsh.

Tim either impressed Walsh quite a bit with his fastball or did something right in that audition room: He ended up landing the part. Not to slight his pitching arm, but the credit probably goes to his acting talent. His tape, in which he begged a ranch hand to keep Skyrocket away from him, hit a home run in its own way, displaying a natural vulnerability far beyond most of the other kiddie actors of the day.

Tim, however, couldn't settle for the job offer as it was. He told Uncle Sam—his family-friend agent, Sam Armstrong—"I don't wanna play that rich, snotty guy. I'd rather be somebody like that other guy, his friend in it, Spin. He's cool."

"Spin's a very small part," Uncle Sam told him. "That will never do." But with an eye toward pleasing his fourteen-year-old client, Sam called the Disney representatives to play hardball. "My guy wants to be in this but he doesn't want to be Marty," he told them. "He wants to be Spin, if Spin is an equal-sized character." The casting, as it turned out, made more sense; Tim's easygoing confidence fit more with Spin than with Marty. So producers, enamored enough of Tim to rearrange the show dynamics a bit, adjusted the script to give Spin equal time.

They still, however, needed a Marty. "And my memory is that I suggested Dave Stollery for Marty," Tim says now. "Though I just read something where somebody else said their mother suggested Dave Stollery." That's Lonnie Burr: "I read for Marty and didn't get it, but there was a guy, David Stollery, who was typed the way I was," Lonnie recalls. "We were always the rich, snotty kids who were intellectuals. So I had been up against him for things, and my mom happened to be an agent at that time. And when I didn't get it, she called up David's mom." But Tim insists, good-naturedly: "I think I did, and I've always told him that I'm totally responsible for his career."

As for David, he supports his longtime onscreen partner's story. Tim's account of how *he* got his friend the gig, David says, "annoyed my mother forever till the day she passed on" because she insisted she'd gotten it for him herself. "But I have to believe," David says. "Don't ever tell Tim I said this, but he's an amazing guy. And when he says that he put in a word for me, I believe him, because Tim has always been well connected."

However it came to be, soon the buddies were living out the boyish dream life of spending their days on a real ranch, surrounded by more than a dozen supporting young actors and lots of real horses.

As production on the new series geared up, Walt Disney himself made an appearance at the ranch to play a few possible theme songs and let the cast vote on which they liked best. "Mr. Disney was very good at working with children," David says. "He was very good at bringing you in so you felt you had a say and got a piece of the action."

The boys also got to learn to ride horses and perform most of their own stunts. The producers asked them if they knew how to ride, to which, naturally, they replied, "Oh, sure." They would've said they could drive a submarine if they'd been asked to. "You know kids at that age," David says. "Of course we didn't." As luck would have it, Disney sent David and Tim out to riding lessons anyway, wise to their exaggerated accounts of their skills. "They taught us to cowpoke and to mount and dismount bareback," David recalls. "Though just to ride and keep yourself from falling off the damn horse at full gallop was enough." Adds Tim, "They virtually gave us our horses. That made it more personal and fun, which helped because they soon found we weren't that good."

Once shooting began, their days grew long. "Overall it was a tough grind because we had to be at Buena Vista Studios at like seven o'clock in the morning," David remembers. "From there we got on buses for an hour-and-a-half ride out to Placerita Canyon to the Golden Oak Ranch." They started filming the show during the summer to avoid school conflicts, but that meant facing Southern California desert weather at its hottest, with highs in the nineties. They'd shoot all day in the summer sun, then take the bus back, drive home from there, put cold cream on their makeup- and dust-caked faces, and memorize lines for the next day, just to wake up the following morning and do it all over again. And during those summer months, they'd film six days out of seven for a forty-eight-hour workweek—eight hours a day, plus transit.

The difficult circumstances, however, rolled off the resilient kids' backs, even as they noticed the crew wilting under the pressure. "It was a lot of fun because you were out there with the horses and you could go and screw off between shots," David says. "But the poor assistant director is trying to keep teenage boys out of trouble, which is an impossible task. They're the ones who really had the headaches. It's like trying to herd cats. I don't know what they paid those gentlemen, but no matter what it wasn't enough."

In the end, the hard work—and hard play—paid off. As part of the *Mickey Mouse Club* phenomenon, *Spin and Marty* exploded to massive popularity, getting more fan mail than even cultural sensation Davy Crockett. Whether you called it a mini-miniseries or one of TV's first teen dramas, *Spin and Marty* generated fan response like nothing other than Annette could. Even the most popular Mouseketeer of all fell for Spin. "In my adoration of Tim, I was one of millions of teenage girls," Annette writes in her autobiography. Sadly, Tim never knew that Annette—who was becoming an idol in her own right—entertained any particular interest in him, but it's likely her enthusiasm would've made the reluctant heartthrob blush at the time. "It was always an embarrassment to me that people made such a big fuss about me," Tim says. "I was always very strongly opinionated, but I was not showy, and to be put in the spotlight was not my favorite thing. But it's a nice thing to actually have been a part of something that apparently meant a lot to a lot of people."

By December 1955, Tim and David found themselves summoned to Disneyland to sign autographs along with Annette, who was getting far more fan mail now than the rest of her fellow Mouseketeers. After changing into their autograph-signing gear for the day—Tim and David in jeans and T-shirts, Annette in her Mouseketeer version of a cowgirl outfit—Disney staffers carted the kids out to where they'd meet their fans. The trio of teen idols found thousands of people waiting. "Who are they?" Tim asked his cohorts, with genuine fear. "Why are they here? What do they *want?*"

Facing crowds of admirers, however, soon became just another day at the office for the budding stars. A *hard* day. "We'd sit there and sign autographs and have a little repartee with the fans," David says. "That's tough work because, you know, it's one thing to be polite and behave yourself for ten minutes, but it's another to do it for six, eight hours a day for two weeks and not make any slip-ups. My mother would always be reminding me, 'This is public and you're getting paid for this and you cannot make any mistakes. There are no do-overs.' It was probably the most valuable training and discipline I received."

Their massive popularity mystified them, even at the time. They knew their serial was no cause for acclaim by anything other than kiddie-TV standards—and were a little shocked to find themselves with such a passionate fan base. "Neither of us had been on a series, and we didn't comprehend the power of the repeat viewer," David says. "When we realized how popular it was, we went, 'My God,' because we knew that we weren't in any great theatrical production. We understood that it was entertainment, kind of this cheesy show geared to the lowest common denominator of the audience. And yet there was this tremendous reaction to it."

It charmed its way into a cherished place in viewers' hearts despite often-clunky dialogue and sometimes obvious, sometimes poky, storytelling. "I've often said that I don't think it was that good, really," Tim says. "But it struck a nerve with so many kids because it was novel. Kids' TV was all cartoons or puppet shows until *Spin and Marty* and *The Mickey Mouse Club*."

Just as kids across the country were snapping up their own Mouse ears and singing "The Mickey Mouse Club March," now boys were also buzzing their hair to look like the ever-cool Spin. "Apparently Rick Nelson and I popularized the flattop," Tim recalls.

"A lot of parents told me that, and that their kids could handle getting braces because I had braces. [Disney] had wanted to know if I'd take them off, and I said no. Apparently that assuaged a lot of kids who were about to have braces."

While the steady schedule of shooting and public appearances didn't allow the boys much time for typical teenage recreation, their steady paychecks enabled both of the nascent automotive enthusiasts—who'd first bonded over Tim's toy car—to buy their first vehicles. Tim purchased a "snazzy" Alfa Romeo before he even had a driver's license, so for a while he could drive his luxury sports car only while supervised by a licensed driver. "I had a learner's permit, so I could drive it to the studio with my babysitter," he says. "The argument with my mother was that it was my own money. I could do it myself. And the thing was, I didn't really have time for anything except work and my car." David even drew Tim a portrait of the car, so he could admire it on the wall even when he couldn't be near it.

David, for his part, bought a BMW 360cc Boxer Twin motorcycle that he was so protective of, he kept it in his bedroom, bringing it out only to shuttle to his neighborhood girlfriend's house and back. He felt the indulgence was the least he was entitled to after his years of working in the entertainment industry. "I was a very inexpensive child to raise," David says. "I bought all my clothes. I made all my own allowances. I bought all my motorcycles."

The Mouseketeers, too, were struggling to juggle the increasingly disparate parts of their showbiz-kid lives. But their Mousehood presented a very particular set of challenges to which not even their own Spin and Marty could relate: competing with two dozen cast mates on a daily basis while facing the constant threat of being fired and replaced; handling the outsized popularity of one particular Mouse; and doing it all under the influence of not just their own adolescent hormones, but a classroom's worth of other kids' as well.

Part 2

THE SHOW YEARS

Chapter Seven

The Ex-Mouseketeers' Club

Mary Espinosa's mother sat her down in her brand-new living room for a talk, the little girl's curly hair limp and her chubby cheeks flushed from a long day of performing at Disneyland. The eleven-year-old had just used her earnings from her first season on *The Mickey Mouse Club* to move her family of nine from the East Los Angeles housing project where they'd been living to a four-bedroom stucco ranch house in the growing suburb of La Puente. Now, however, Mary had to face some bad news: As producers had told her mother in Disney parlance, Mary's contract *would not be renewed.* The little girl didn't understand at first: *What did that even mean?* The answer, her mother went on to explain: She was no longer part of the club that's made for you and me. She was *being kicked out.*

"Once the first year was in the can, and once we opened Disneyland, I feel like our function was looked at differently," Mary says. "Then they saw that some people were getting a lot of fan mail and some weren't, and they dropped the people who weren't. It was real simple." As time went on, she came to understand, that her place in the Mouseketeer hierarchy had never quite been secure. "I have a picture of Dik Darley directing me, and I must not have been doing it right," she says. "Because I don't look happy and neither does he. I know I was a little late coming into the dances and stuff. I kind of did my own thing."

However, the firing still came as a devastating blow. She'd been able to get her family out of the projects by providing the down payment on their home, which gave them manageable mortgage bills even without her Mouseketeer income, but that barely registered as something to be proud of in her sixth-grade world. She had what she considered far bigger problems—namely, returning to school an *ex*-Mouseketeer, the very picture of rejection in her own young mind. She refused to talk about her time on *The Mickey Mouse Club* with her classmates. "I was a little ashamed, a little embarrassed," she remembers. "I was involved in music—I was always in the choir and the jazz groups, and performed in plays and musicals—but we didn't really discuss that I'd been a Mouseketeer. My teachers knew; we just didn't talk about it."

Worst of all, Mary didn't realize until much later—because she never returned to the studio lot—that she wasn't the only Mouseketeer to lose her ears that day. In a first-season-ending housecleaning, fifteen Mice were fired, including Dallas Johann's brother, John Lee, who'd never found his footing on the show after stepping in for his camera-shy younger sibling. "The kids they kept had a lot more experience than I did," John says. "They all were backed by very strong show-business parents. I remember being directed in one scene and the director was trying to get me to do something and it wasn't coming out right." As a result, he says, "I never got to do much on the show after I was hired. It was a traumatic experience for me. You want to be special, you want to be good, and then you find out you're not." (Like his brother, though, he'd go on to have a successful dance career, first with original *Mickey Mouse Club* choreographer Burch Mann's professional troupe, then on Broadway, including Stephen Sondheim's *Follies*. He's since retired to upstate New York, where he lived with his author wife of ten years, H. B. Gilmour, until her death in 2009, and continues to perform in local plays and poetry readings.)

Producers, having learned their lesson from their earlier missteps, kept just three Mouseketeers under the age of twelve, and never hired any boys that young again to avoid troubles like they had early on with Paul Petersen and the Rooney brothers. Contracts for new hires switched from seven-year commitments with six-month options to one-year commitments with three-month options. It turned out the Mouseketeers' early, harsh lesson in the fragility of employment—back when Dallas Johann, Paul Petersen, and the Rooney brothers had been fired before the show even aired—was only the beginning of their job security worries. The revolving door of firing and recasting would never quite stop at *The Mickey Mouse Club*. And it would shake up more little Mouse lives than fans ever knew.

*   *   *

After the mass firing, the remaining ten Mouseketeers weren't safe either. Their beloved director, Dik Darley, had been dismissed as well, and the man who'd come to take his place, Sid Miller, was making them re-audition to be allowed to return for the second season. When the surviving Mice performed for Miller at the end of the first season in hopes of keeping their spots in the cast for the second, Tommy stumbled. Miller asked him to dance, and Tommy explained that he'd never been that good at it but he was a really good singer and Dik Darley had always been fine with him just sort of faking it off to the side.... But Miller wouldn't look past Tommy's one shortcoming the way Darley had. To make matters worse, Tommy's high soprano was changing. "I had a break in my voice," he says. "And the casting director said, 'You know you're not going to be asked back unless your voice gets better.'"

Tommy struck a bargain with Miller and the ever-more-impatient producers: He would learn to dance and smooth out his voice over the coming summer before the second season began, or he'd turn in his Mouse ears for good. He'd spend his entire hiatus in the dance studio and with his voice teacher. "So for about a month and a half," he says, "I just concentrated on lessons like crazy."

Tommy returned to the set that second season still aching from months of dance classes. "I had to re-audition on this huge stage," he recalls. "Not one fixture on it, except there was one big light. One of those stands with the big bulb. And there was the director, executive producer, casting director, and the choreographer. Those four people. I came in and I was all ready to sing, I had some music with me...but there was no piano. They said, 'okay, sing.' So, okay, I sang. Without music. And I was ready to do a little dance, so I did a little tap dance. Without music."

They thanked him and sent him outside the theater with his mother while they deliberated about his fate. "And about five minutes later [Miller] came out and said, 'You're back on the show,'" Tommy says. "It was nerve-wracking but it was kind of neat. It paid off, and I then stayed on the show. And I didn't miss any of the show."

He could stay, making him one of the few non-trained dancers remaining in the cast. He would even stay on the Red Team. Once again his voice had saved him—and his dancing was now at least passable, if by no means a guarantee of continued future employment. "I was a faker as a dancer," Tommy says. "I looked like I was making the steps. Thank God for Lonnie, Bobby, and Sharon; those three really helped me a lot, dancing-wise. They'd get me over to the side and teach me."

Those who survived those first-season cuts soon had another kind of uncertainty to face: As production on the second season revved up, a brigade of four brand-new Mouseketeers marched onto the set to take the place of those who'd been dismissed.

Sherry Alberoni came to *The Mickey Mouse Club* as a huge fan of the first season. She'd watched religiously ("I had the little plastic ears and I sat in front of the TV," she says) and preferred it to *Howdy Doody* and *Pinky Lee* (on which she'd appeared once). Even before she auditioned for the show, she felt confident she could be a Mouse if she wanted to. "All kids dreamed, literally dreamed, that we could be Mouseketeers," she says. "Every kid in America thought they *could*, because the Mouseketeers were normal."

In her case, she was right—she won a precious set of her own, authentic, one-hundred-percent-felt Mouse ears thanks to her unusual audition: She played the trumpet while tap-dancing. The nine-year-old with a shy smile and a lisp—who changed her last name to the less-ethnic Allen when she joined the Mouseketeers— had only recently begun her show-business career at the prodding of her aunt, a former vaudeville dancer. "It sounded exciting, like, 'Wow, Hollywood, I've always wanted to see Hollywood,'" Sherry says. "It wasn't a thing where it was like, 'If you don't get this job, you don't eat tonight.' My dad brought the bacon home, my mom cooked it. [Auditioning] was just like a plaything, going and getting in costumes. I loved to dance, loved to sing, loved to show off."

She also brought an innate confidence to the job that had been on display at one of the first auditions of her career, a year before she joined *The Mickey Mouse Club*, when she was forced to defend her lisp to none other than *I Love Lucy*'s Desi Arnaz. "He laughed at me," she recalls. "He called in his secretary, telling her, 'You've got to hear this—this is the funniest thing I've ever heard!' He had that thick Cuban accent and I could barely understand him. After a while he was making such a big deal about it, and laughing so much to my face, that I looked up at him and said, 'Well, at least I can speak English!' And I turned and walked out." The two eventually got the chance to make nice: "Years later, at another audition, I reminded him of that," Sherry says. "He laughed and said, 'I loved that! I told everybody in the world about you!'"

Eileen Diamond, on the other hand, brought a quiet poise to the cast thanks to her extensive dance training. She had blown off the mass auditions for *The Mickey Mouse Club* the year before, when all of her classmates at Doreen Tracey's father's dance studio had gone. She wasn't sure what this Mouseketeer business was going to be all about, so the thirteen-year-old had skipped the tryouts to stick with her tap and piano lessons instead. But when she heard Disney was looking for new cast members a year later, she decided to go out for it this time. She was one of the few kids in America who still hadn't watched the show, but she couldn't help knowing how famous Doreen and the rest of the gang were because of it. "I wasn't really sure what it was," she says. "All I knew was that it was a Mickey Mouse thing, and they wore ears."

Though she'd never been on a television show before, she won choreographer Tommy Mahoney over with her impressive leg extension when she performed a ballet piece, then won the rest of the audition panel over by singing "Over the Rainbow," complete with Judy Garland braids. Once they told her she'd made the cast, she still had no idea what she was in for, both because she had no TV experience and because she'd yet to tune in to the actual show. "I knew nothing about it," she says. "When they called me and said, 'We want to put you under contract,' I ran and put on the TV and watched for the first time."

Perhaps because she knew Doreen from the dance studio, or perhaps because she was just a levelheaded kid who wanted nothing more than to spend her days performing, joining the biggest kiddie show to hit television didn't faze Eileen much. "What's so funny, when I think back on it now, is that I was so nonchalant," she says. "It wasn't any big deal. I just thought, 'Oh, that's what I get to do, and I'll do that.' I didn't think much about it. It was like you take your classes, you take your voice lessons and drama, and now you're just doing it in front of a camera."

Jay-Jay Solari, however, felt the gravity of joining the biggest kid show in the nation, mainly because he arrived on the set under serious pressure from his stage mother to make the most of his first big shot at stardom. The twelve-year-old scored a spot with his natural tap-dancing, which he'd taken up back in his hometown of Boston when his mom, alarmed by his penchant for throwing rocks at the windows of a nearby factory building to pass the time, sought to keep him busy and out of trouble. "Seeing a potential sniper in her midst, and the war being over and Hitler now deceased, my mother decided perhaps some less deadly diversion might be in order for her budding assassin," Jay-Jay told website OriginalMMC.com, in an interview he says is his final, definitive word on his Mouseketeer days. "I was taken to dancing school and could tap dance as though I had been learning it for twenty years. It's just—like throwing rocks accurately—something I can do."

Though he'd appeared in a play with Vincent Price and in a Sid Caesar variety show at the Boston Gardens, he was intimidated by the prospect of joining the famous Mouseketeers as his first job after his starstruck mother moved the family to Los Angeles. "I had absolutely no business being involved in any of this show-business crap," he said. "I wanted to go out and play guns. That's all I ever wanted to do. Play guns." But for now, he'd be one of the newest Mouseketeers, whether he liked it or not.

Cheryl Holdridge, a stunning blond ballerina, wanted nothing more than to be a Mouseketeer. She had auditioned for a part in *The Mickey Mouse Club*'s *Hardy Boys* serial, and when she didn't get it she begged her agent to get her a shot at Mousehood instead. But her agent wouldn't set it up, thinking Cheryl—who'd danced the lead in *The Nutcracker Suite* at L.A.'s Greek Theatre for two years running—could make more money elsewhere.

At first Cheryl played along with that logic, but eventually the twelve-year-old's competitive spirit got the best of her when Sherry, a longtime family friend, told her she'd gotten a spot on the show. "I had this girlfriend, and she told me she was going to be a Mouseketeer," Cheryl said in a 1979 interview. "Well, that did it. I wasn't going to have some friend of mine being a Mouseketeer and not me, so, unbeknownst to my mother and my agent, I rang up Lee Travers at Disney and arranged to come over for an interview."

Like Darlene before her, she sang "The Ballad of Davy Crockett."

Once again, it proved a lucky audition song—at least, eventually. "It was a terrifying experience," Cheryl said. "Afterward, I was called up to the table to talk and I couldn't think of anything to say. I just knew I had blown it, and I guess my mother did too, because I remember she was very sweet to me in the car on the way home." And yet: "A few days later I got a call to report to the studio."

When the quartet of new Mice arrived for their first day at the studio, they found themselves plunked into the middle of a number that the established Mouseketeers had already been rehearsing. Jay-Jay melted into a puddle of awe. "I go into this room and there's all the Mouseketeers," he said. "These icons I used to envy, and then I'm entering a room with them already doing some dance together to learn. I go, 'Uh-oh.'"

Sherry, however, found facing down her new coworkers as easy as standing up to Desi Arnaz. Even Annette, whom she'd admired every day on television the previous year, didn't shake her rock-solid self-assurance. "I guess it was because I knew their names," she says. "I felt like we were all friends. They were in my living room every day, right?" It helped that she had appeared on a few other children's shows as well. Even though she had a special place in her heart for the Mouseketeers: "It was just another show to me. I had done some other show the week before. The only difference was I liked the idea of being around all *these* kids. *That* was fun." In fact, she reveled in learning from the kids she'd once idolized.

"I really looked up to Darlene," Sherry says. "She was so talented, and she kind of took me under her wing. And Bobby was always helping me with the dance steps. Just the nicest guy."

The new kids were given strange costumes to change into—not the familiar *Mickey Mouse Club* uniforms they'd been expecting, but clothes to reflect their roles in a skit about traveling to faraway lands. "They got us all dressed up and threw us into it," Eileen says. "I played a little photographer, it was some type of travel piece with a boat and things like that." No one explained a thing to them about the basics of set life, either—for instance, the fact that ringing bells indicate when the crew should be quiet because film is rolling, and when they can relax because it's stopped. So Sound Stage 1 itself felt more like a foreign country to them than anything they were singing about in the skit. "I do remember it was the first time I heard bells on a soundstage," Eileen says. "I didn't know what they meant. I was really a rookie."

The new Mouseketeers had to jump right into the now high-stakes, fast-moving, all-encompassing endeavor that *The Mickey Mouse Club* had become. "Having a job at twelve is like having a job at forty," Jay-Jay said. "You have to do stuff. There's a ton of money involved. It's big business, and with Walt Disney it's—at least when he was alive—big business of an innovative and revolutionary nature." Sherry's mother, for one, swooped in to keep her daughter's perspective in check. "My mom told me, 'You're no different than any girl who babysits,'" Sherry recalls. "'Some kids have a newspaper route, some kids mow lawns, some kids babysit.

You're no different, no better, and the only reason that you ever get a job is because God wants you to get the job.'"

They did everything that was asked of them—Eileen even got a perm to please the producers. "They wanted to give a permanent to my hair so it held the curls more, so it had more body," Eileen remembers. "I had very long hair, and I wore it mostly pulled back in a long, low ponytail. Already somebody had braids, and they wanted to make everybody different." Jay-Jay worked hard enough that, despite his early jitters, he earned a coveted spot in the Roll Call, as did Cheryl. Even so, Jay-Jay knew he didn't belong. "I had no business being there," he said. "I couldn't do what Bobby did, because he did all sorts of weird stuff. Sharon, on the other hand, was a blur of a tap dancer, plus she had all this 'projection.' I hated projecting. I hated performing."

Eventually, it showed, and Jay-Jay was on his way out, as were Eileen and Sherry, who got lost in the shuffle of joining the show mid-phenomenon. Just months after arriving on the set, Sherry, Eileen, and Jay-Jay, along with Charley Laney, Larry Larsen, Dennis Day, and Margene Storey would become the next wave of ex-Mouseketeers, cut before the third season was about to begin. Producers wanted to make more stars like Annette, who was becoming a household name at this point—although they'd settle even for stars of the Lonnie, Doreen, Darlene, and Bobby order. And that meant shunting off the kids who weren't clicking with viewers to make room for more potential teen idols. Fans had taken a liking to Cheryl's sunny demeanor and warm smile, but the rest had to go, sending seven more Mouseketeers the way of Mary Espinosa, Dallas Johann, and so many others. The Ex–*Mickey Mouse Club* now contained twice as many members as the current *Mickey Mouse Club*.

Sherry made a smooth transition, having made fans in important places during her brief run as a Mouse: "I left *The Mickey Mouse Club* on a Friday and went to work for Lou Costello on a Monday morning, so I never had any sense of loss," she says. "Lou Costello's little girl, Carole, used to watch *The Mickey Mouse Club* with her dad, and I was her favorite. He liked my lisp, so he hired me to play his adopted daughter in the last film that him and Bud Abbott made together called *Dance with Me, Henry*."

Eileen, too, took the news in stride: "They didn't know which way they were going with the show, what they were doing," she says. "They kept the more well-known kids who were in the Roll Call. Frankly, I guess I probably was hurt in some way. But I think I was in the thick of the good stuff." (She'd stay in show business though, going on to dance with the New York City Ballet, spending several years as a casting director and a talent agent in Hollywood, and founding a still-thriving arts summer program for kids in central Maine.) Dennis—the kid who'd survived two seasons without knowing how to sing—remained stoic, like any good child performer. As he said in an interview in 1971, "My mother kept telling me how to react to hurt and frustration; you didn't. You just didn't react."

Jay-Jay, however, felt the impact. "You can't go down the street to Warner Brothers and apply for a Mouseketeer job, because they don't have any Mouseketeer jobs, and neither does the phone company, nor the supermarket, nor the fry stand," he said. "You had the only Mouseketeer job available. It is what you *are*. Being a Mouseketeer is what you *do*. And you just got *fired*. Why? Maybe because you *suck*. Or maybe not! You see, they never tell you. They never sit you down and explain, 'Jay-Jay, we are firing you because you just don't seem to be fitting in with our corporate view of ourselves, and we can't really promote you because you already had the highest job we offer around here. We feel that moving you over to Shipping would make all the others in Shipping uncomfortable, and we can't really make you a cameraman or a producer because, well, you're only twelve. No offense.' And so you find yourself fired, without even that little sendoff. Without even a letter of recommendation. Because, really, what could they recommend you for?"

Soon, though, Walt Disney Studios was looking for still *more* new Mice, ever more desperate to find breakout stars who could propel the hit for seasons into the future. Producers even went beyond Los Angeles for this round of open-call auditions, eager to find little Annettes-in-the-rough to take the place of the most recent castoffs. Now, with ratings dropping and the most recent round of casting producing only one star, the pressure was on to perk up the flagging hit with new energy if the series was to survive beyond one more season.

Among their audition tour stops was the Cow Palace, a livestock-pavilion-turned-arena just outside San Francisco, where the five hundred or so hopefuls milling about under the concrete-and-steel roof included one devoted thirteen-year-old fan named Don Agrati. He'd watched the Mouseketeers every day throughout the past few seasons and had come that day to try his luck at the behest of his dance teacher. "The Mouseketeers were like the biggest thing in those days," he remembers now. "I couldn't wait to get home from school and watch the show. I was so into it."

The swelling crowd of wannabe Mouseketeers overwhelmed Don, because anybody who could do anything—from twirl a Popsicle stick to tap and twirl professionally—had shown up, thrilled by the prospect of appearing before big-time Hollywood producers. That didn't happen every day in Northern California, where kids who had agents and résumés were the exception rather than the rule. Don watched, enthralled, as one girl in a glittery dress with a hem that unfurled and recurled with every perfect turn swooshed through a routine like she'd been dancing longer than she could've been alive. "I thought, 'Oh, she's going to get it,'" he says. "I just thought she was beautiful, she was going to be a Mouseketeer."

Then again, he didn't lack talent himself. He could dance in addition to playing a whopping six instruments—accordion, clarinet, bass, drums, guitar, and trumpet. He would strum and pound and blow a mere handful of those at his audition, so used to showing them all off that afterward he wouldn't even remember which three or four he'd played. He did a tap dance as well.

He got through to the next round, for which the studio flew him down to Los Angeles for a meeting with Walt Disney—the boss always had final approval on the chosen Mouseketeers, but because the audition net had been cast wider this time, candidates had to travel from across the country to see him. Don, however, still wasn't sure he had the part yet, as another kid, whose name was Buster, had gotten the same golden ticket from the auditions. No one had said that only one of them could make it, but Don assumed it was a winner-take-all situation.

Don and Buster soon found themselves facing off on a hardwood floor, perfect for tap-dancing, at the Disney lot in Burbank. Buster's routine went flawlessly, clacking in perfect rhythm on that shiny floor. But when Don's turn came, something went awry: For some reason, the piano player kept changing tempos, and Don couldn't keep up. It was the same routine he'd done when he was so great at the Cow Palace, but now he could feel it getting away from him… and *oh, no, why was that piano guy speeding up again?*

Don got through his audition, but he knew his performance was off. Then, as he answered producers' questions about why he wanted to be a Mouseketeer and what his range of talents was, something else happened: The Mouseketeers themselves walked in. They just scurried through, eight or nine of them, on their way to do whatever it was they did, doubtlessly something important, a taping or a performance or whatever it was that made them have to smell so magical—like pancake makeup and lipstick and hairspray, like dreams. Annette, she floated right there among them. Don stopped cold just to watch them pass by.

And then they disappeared behind the door, the interrogation ended, and Mr. Disney went over and shook Buster's and his father's hands. "It was just wonderful what you did," he told Buster. "Terrific." The mustachioed mogul looked across the room at Don and his mother, dismissing them with just a "Very good, thank you very much." He turned and walked out of the room. Don was sure he'd blown it.

But after a dejected plane trip home, a miracle: The Disney producers called. Don Agrati would become a Mouseketeer. That harrowing final round of auditions? They were just testing him; they wanted to know if he could handle being upstaged, since he'd be joining a cast that was already full of stars in their own right. "Isn't that wild?" Don says. "Poor Buster."

All of a sudden Don found himself whisked from his normal life in the small Northern California town of Lafayette to living in the Hollywood Hotel with his mom and sharing a school trailer with the same kids he'd watched on TV every day for two years.

Getting a job on *The Mickey Mouse Club*, however, meant changing everything in his thus far normal, suburban existence—including uprooting his family to move 357 miles south. His father soon gave up the family salami business, the one Don had always expected to take over someday, and joined them in Los Angeles, loath to let such a seemingly impossible opportunity—joining the cast of a hit Disney show!—escape his talented son. Mr. Agrati would take jobs selling used cars and driving bakery trucks, staking the family's future on his son's job, the one that paid more than his grown-man jobs ever did. "That was an amazing sacrifice," Don says. "I have to thank him. I never really did thank him. My show-business career could've been over as fast as it happened."

Meanwhile, Don met the rest of the new "freshman class": Bonnie Lynn Fields—a thirteen-year-old blond dancer and singer who went by just "Lynn"—had, like Don, been a faithful fan. She'd been aiming for just a onetime Talent Round-Up appearance and ended up a full-fledged Mouse. Linda Hughes, a ten-year-old who auditioned in San Diego, tap-danced and baton-twirled her way onto the show and would end up Don's regular duet partner. And Lynn Ready—there really were three kids with almost the same name in this new batch of Mouseketeers, although this one was a boy—moved from Dallas to join *The Mickey Mouse Club* thanks to the twelve-year-old's singing and dancing skills as well as his steel-guitar and piano playing. Together, they brought the total Mouse roster to fourteen.

Early on, Annette, Cheryl, Doreen, and Sharon noticed the new boy Don—who, even though he was a few years younger than they were, already had the cleft chin and perfect cheekbones that would later make him a teen idol when he starred on *My Three Sons*. The girls circled around him and cooed, "We think you're really cute." Annette kissed his smooth, tan forehead. "That was it, I died and went to heaven, Mouseketeer heaven," Don says. "That was kind of my welcome into the group." Young Don didn't know just how cute Doreen thought he was: "To this day I still have a crush on Donnie," she says. "But he was too young. That's not proper."

Don's journey through Mouseketeer heaven continued when he got to make his first trip to Disneyland as an actual part of the Main Street Parade. "All these kids, they were paying attention to Annette and Cubby and Karen and Doreen and Darlene, but it didn't matter to me," Don says. "We would march down Main Street and go over to Tomorrowland, and they had a stage set up there and we would do like two or three or four talent shows during the day. Then a couple of the Mouseketeers who were my age—Karen, Cubby, and Bonnie—would take me and show me Disneyland [after hours]. Sometimes we'd have the whole park to ourselves."

As the new faces infiltrated *The Mickey Mouse Club* onscreen, first-season castoff Mary Espinosa was carrying on with her painfully *regular* life without Mouseketeerdom after her unceremonious dismissal nearly two years earlier. Like a girl invited to join the most elite of the popular kids, then cast away and reduced to watching them have fun across the schoolyard, she tuned in to the show, on occasion, from the house she'd purchased for her family with her Mouseketeer earnings. She could stand just a peek at a time to check on her former friends—as well as the kids she didn't get to know well but wished she had. She watched as her onetime castmates danced and sang and laughed and cheered with new friends, without her. The rejection of being let go still stung enough that she couldn't watch a full episode more than once in a great while. "I'd peek at it to see these great new kids and wish I'd gotten to know them," she says. "It was weird to see the original ones growing up and growing into adults: Annette looked like a beautiful Barbie doll at some point, and I was like, 'Wow! I knew her!'"

Dealing with such bittersweet feelings—and painful rejection—left many former Mouseketeers disillusioned about the magical world of Disney in a way the fans watching from their homes would never know. But the Mice also faced the kind of difficulties so many kids their age, so many of their fans, faced growing up outside the spotlight. All the Disney-bred discipline in the world couldn't stop puberty and young love from coloring everything that happened on set—and, occasionally, on camera—as the Mice ventured deeper into their teen years.

Chapter Eight

First Kisses, Spin the Bottle, and Too-Tight Sweaters

Adolescence Comes to the Set

Lonnie Burr wanted to give Annette Funicello a token of his affection, and unlike most of the longing boys in her growing fan base, he actually knew her. He was even going steady with her for the whole first season of their show. And as the first year of *The Mickey Mouse Club* wound down, the time had come to give her his ring, like any guy would give any girl in school. Of course, since they didn't go to the kind of school that had its own rings, he opted for a simple gold band on a gold chain instead.

The hour-long ride between Disneyland in Anaheim and the studio in Burbank ignited *The Mickey Mouse Club*'s first romantic sparks when Lonnie's and Annette's moms decided to carpool for their kids' weekend appearances at the park. From when they first met on the set, Lonnie says he "immediately focused on Annie" among all the girls in the cast. One night, Lonnie made his signature move in the dark backseat of his parents' car on the way home from Orange County: He grabbed Annette's hand. She squeezed back. For months to come, they intertwined their fingers as their mothers drove. "We did *a lot* of hand-holding," Lonnie says. "And it was very dark in the backseat." Annette fell for Lonnie's cuteness—and, of course, his coolness—enough to give him her prized first kiss. "We really were an item," he says. "We weren't going out with anyone else. Going steady then, it was a big deal."

Now that he had America's Sweetheart, he knew he had to hold on to her. So to seal the deal, Lonnie presented Annie with the symbolic ring during a Mouseketeer party. The way Annette remembers it in her memoir, she would throw the ring at him during several angsty lovers' quarrels until one day she got tired of throwing it and that was the end of their romance. Lonnie recalls the ring's return as even more dramatic: The other girl Mice, he says, started oohing and aahing over it at a gathering that included their parents, alerting Annette's dad to its presence—and significance. Soon, the thick brick wall known as Joe Funicello was standing between Annie and Lonnie. Joe demanded his daughter return the gift; always the good girl, she did. They were through, whether it was because of her dad, as Lonnie said, or because of their fights, as Annette said.

It made sense, in a way, that Annette and Lonnie would be the first on-set couple. Lonnie fancied himself quite the ladies' man. "I think he thought so," Cubby quips. "I'm not sure the ladies thought so." Actually, as much as Lonnie's male costars rolled their eyes at his smooth act, it did work quite well on some of the ladies. "He was adorable," Mary says. "He was smart. He was twelve going on twenty." Doreen likens Lonnie's teen persona to James Bond: "He was smart and dapper and together, darling, together."

Annie and Lonnie's puppy love may have been the first blush of romance to color the set of *The Mickey Mouse Club*, but it was only the beginning of the adolescent changes that would wash over the Mice during their time on the set. The Mouseketeers' childhoods would include the most ordinary of moments, such as first loves stifled by protective parents, experimental first sips of liquor, and blossoming bodies. But those typical teen moments would often be enlarged and distorted by the lens of growing stardom, with those first loves becoming unattainable star-crushes to millions, those first sips of liquor taken not at school dances but on cross-country publicity tours, and those blossoming bodies inviting nationally televised scrutiny.

Aside from Annette and Lonnie's relationship, the first trickle of romances to hit the set weren't all that real: There was the rumored kiss between Annette and Bobby behind the school trailer, though that turned out to be nothing more than untrue gossip spread by the mischievous John Lee Johann. "I was twelve years old," he says by way of explanation. "And I actually didn't just make it up. They did come out from behind there very conspicuously together—it just turned out not to be what they were doing."

But John Lee wasn't the only one making up stories about not-quite-true romances. The studio grew increasingly fond of what it called "building crushes" among the cast. The Disney publicists, for instance, tried to pair Dennis Day up with Cheryl Holdridge.

The PR machine would start rumors, Dennis said in a 1971 interview, and encourage hand-holding on the lot. But Dennis, in this case, was having none of what plenty of other boys in America would've given anything for; he was annoyed by Cheryl's ability to always get her smile perfect on the first take in publicity shots when they posed together. Teen magazines got in on the "couples" act too, throwing parties and arranging for young stars to be seen on "dates"—which were, in fact, just elaborate photo ops with little to do with real-life relationships. "They'd say, 'Okay, we'll put this one and this one together on a date,'" Sharon recalls, "and then a photographer would go with them and shoot it."

Many of the real on-set attempts at coupling fizzled out fast. Doreen, who was blossoming into a curvy, stunning redhead, didn't need the publicity department to get her dates, though she burned through crushes fast. First she went out with Tim Considine, that swaggering kid from *Spin and Marty* who'd join the Mouseketeers once in a while for photo shoots and publicity appearances. "I had a crush on Timmy," Doreen says. "The whole nation did." Then she dated Lonnie, though they quickly shifted to friendship instead. Tommy Cole and Sharon went steady for a couple of weeks once, during which Tommy wooed her by getting her favorite candy, Butter Brickle, from the studio-lot vending machine and leaving it on her desk in the classroom trailer. Sharon went with *Hardy Boys* serial star Tommy Kirk as well, reaching the heights of their commitment when they became blood brother and sister by pricking their index fingers and smooshing them together. For most *Mickey*

Mouse Club "couples," just working together every day served as their "dates," and they never even had to go anywhere off the lot to consider themselves "going out."

Cubby and Karen spent so much time together off the set that they became an exclusive onscreen pair as well. Just thirteen days apart in age, they shared riding and swimming and dancing lessons. They spent their lunches playing canasta together. Cubby spent the night with Karen and her parents on New Year's Eve. *Spin and Marty*'s David Stollery, a talented artist, drew them a picture of the Colonial-style dream house they thought they'd live in with their own family someday. "We just were together, and obviously somebody thought it was fine so they kept putting us together on the show then too," Karen says. "I even heard that we got the most mail aside from Annette. There were a lot of little kids who liked watching us together."

However, despite the fact that many fans would always think of them as a "couple," Cubby and Karen never thought of each other in any romantic sense. Cubby was, well, distracted by the older girls in the cast. "Karen and I were the youngest and together all the time," he says. "But of course I was in love with Annette, Doreen, and Darlene—all those girls who were becoming women. They always thought I was copping a feel or something, but I just liked being around them."

And Karen had her own young love life to occupy her. While John Lee Johann had nursed a secret crush on her before his second-season departure—"I was too young to do anything about it," he says, "a very young twelve"—Karen also entertained a budding romance that would've shocked the millions of fans who thought Cubby was her first true love. When Don Agrati joined the cast, he and Karen developed what Karen calls "a very bad crush" on each other. "I fell in love with Mouseketeer Karen," Don remembers. "We would hold hands in the back of the car without her mother knowing about it."

As for Annette, after her Lonnie liaison, she became notorious on set for her never-ending string of untouchable crushes. If Annette had a fatal flaw, it was a weakness for cute guys. "Annette was boy-crazy," Bobby says. "She'd be in love with Lonnie, a cameraman, Paul Anka...." She covered her loose-leaf binder in doodles of famous male names: Elvis Presley, Tab Hunter, Guy Williams (star of Disney's *Zorro* series). She dedicated an entire inside page to "Frankie"—Avalon, the teen pop star who would later become her onscreen partner in her *Beach Party* movies—in giant, bold, cursive lettering. She dotted the "I" with a heart, surrounded by floating names of his hit songs: "Ginger Bread," "Bobby Sox to Stockings," "Just Ask Your Heart, "Venus," "Too Young to Love."

She dedicated the perimeter of her dressing-room mirror, however, to photos of nothing but Guy Williams. He captivated her more than any of her crushes, perhaps because she, in fact, got to see him in the flesh. *Zorro* shot just two doors down from *The Mickey Mouse Club* in Sound Stage 3, and Disney's ban on girls visiting the *Zorro* set—because the cast and crew were, for the most part, guys—did nothing to deter Annette from sneaking over to catch a glimpse of the star. On-set teacher Mrs. Seaman often caught Annette at Sound Stage 3 and scolded her, but the blushing adolescent couldn't help herself. Every time she finagled a new publicity shot of Williams from the studio, she'd be scurrying over to get another autograph and paternal pat on the head from her idol. She even slept with his framed eight-by-ten every night, her mother sneaking in to pry it from her hands to stop her from rolling over onto it. Eventually it did crack, at last bringing an end to, as she says, "sleeping with Zorro."

Annette had a closer brush with real love when she fell for a Disney crewman—hard. As she tells it in her autobiography, it seems probable that she first met him during her *Mickey Mouse Club* years. (He'd send her red roses for her sixteenth birthday, just after the show ended.) To her teen heart, she had fallen in true love, though he was ten years her senior, and their relations strictly innocent. "I'll wait for you until you're old enough," he'd tell her. She'd sneak off the lot with him and ride on the back of his motorcycle, winding up through the Hollywood Hills on Mulholland Drive. Once, though, someone saw them leave the studio together, and a Disney official called Annette's mother to report that if it happened again the man would be fired. Annette's good-girl side took over, and she reluctantly stopped hanging out with him. "I understood," she writes, "and we only saw each other at work after that." A few years later, her heart broke when she heard he had gotten married, the inevitable result of a young girl's romanticized adolescent crush on a much older man.

*   *   *

While crushes simmered and burned out behind the scenes, puberty was making a noticeable onscreen appearance by the end of the second season when the Mice got too big for their Mousekeuniforms. As their teenage hormones switched from a trickle to a flood, Disney memos instructed costume designers to "try larger sweaters" and cameramen to "keep from shooting the girls in profile." Doreen would later say executives made her and Annette wear "silly tight T-shirts under our sweaters to try and flatten us out. Naturally, we used to punch holes in the right places." Darlene backed this up in a 1971 interview: "They wanted you to look flat-chested. We're lucky we didn't all get cancer of the boobs." Breasts became, in fact, a constant preoccupation for the girls. "It wasn't too much fun going to the beach with Doreen," Cheryl recounted in 1976. "She's really stacked. I started to get an inferiority complex about it. Here comes Doreen bopping along in a bikini and me trailing along all wrapped up in a blanket. I could barely fill my top up."

But Annette, because of her particular popularity with fans, took the brunt of the public scrutiny when it came to Mouseketeer breasts. While several of the older female Mice were busy binding themselves, boys across America started to repeat a common refrain: "Let's go home and watch Annette grow!" It would never be easy attention to take for a girl who even fretted about getting "too tall" to be a Mouseketeer anymore, much less too busty. "It's a very difficult transition to move into that area of pop culture where young boys lust after you," says former Mouseketeer Paul Petersen, who went on to watch Annette and the other girls grow up on television with the rest of the nation before becoming a teen idol himself. "No American male my age, who watched the show, didn't remember watching Annette's dramatic—what shall I call it?—flowering."

The boys didn't face nearly as much public scrutiny of their changing bodies, though they didn't escape unscathed. Dennis Day got his first erection on camera, forcing the crew to stop filming to wait until it subsided. "I sure as hell knew *something* was happening, but I wasn't sure what until later one of the older guys took me aside and explained," he recalled. "I was really freaked and mortified."

As such teenage changes became more obvious in the older Mouseketeers, the divide grew between them and the youngest, still preteen, Mice. The gap was particularly noticeable during the third season, when the Mice and their chaperones would often stay at the Disneyland Hotel overnight after their long days at the Orange County park so they wouldn't have to make the drive back up to Los Angeles late at night. "There were really two divisions as far as the social groups in the Mouseketeers," Don recalls. "There were the older kids, which were Lonnie and Annette and Tommy and Sharon and Doreen. And then there were the younger kids, which were Cubby and Karen, me, Lynn, Bonnie, and Linda. So the little kids would be in one room and the older kids would be in the other room. And once in a while the younger kids would sneak into the older kids' party and watch them play spin the bottle."

"From eight to twelve is a big difference psychologically, between us and the other Mouseketeers," Karen says. The older cast members looked after Cubby and Karen like younger siblings, causing the teeny, towheaded Karen, to often protest, "I'm not a baby, you know!"

But Mouseketeers young and old alike could all agree on one thing: Annette had become the undeniable star among them. The attention that male fans paid to her "flowering" was just an offshoot of a much larger Annette phenomenon that would only grow as *The Mickey Mouse Club* went on. And just as sure as her popularity would lead to loads of fan mail, fawning media coverage, and a foray into pop music, it would also lead to jealous rumors and rivalry—and at least as much anxiety for the shy starlet as for her envious costars.

Chapter Nine

Annette, Annette, Annette

If *The Mickey Mouse Club* had its own version of homecoming queen, head cheerleader, *and* Most Likely to Succeed all rolled into one, it was Annette Funicello. "She just had this charismatic thing that you can't explain," Lonnie says, "but you want to watch her." For some of her costars, it was a pleasure just to be near the girl they describe as a rare breed of graceful, worthy, hardworking teen idol. Others could never quite handle the fact that she got such an outsized portion of fans'—and Disney's—attention. In many cases, how any given Mouse related to the most popular girl on set—and in America—defined his or her experience on *The Mickey Mouse Club*, for good and ill.

The relentless adulation, however, often rattled the icon-in-the-making, who seemed sure it would all go away the minute she grew up. Take the time Annette and costar Doreen Tracey were strutting through Disneyland one day, the cool girls having their run of the campus, when they happened past Mr. Disney and some of his executives strolling the other direction. "We were both fourteen,"

Doreen recalls. "And we were feeling very sophisticated. Even if we had to wear the shirts and ears, we knew we were pretty hot. Then here comes Disney and his entourage." Annette and Doreen said hello, like any polite girls would. The men greeted them back. But just before the girls were out of earshot, a man with a crew cut said to Disney, "What do you think of the girls? They're turning out to be very nice young ladies." Not quite out of the Mouseketeers' hearing range, Disney quipped, "They're more for the fathers than the kids on this show."

While Doreen squealed with glee that the executives had noticed them—"I thought, 'Oh, wow, we're growing up, we'll get a bigger and better part'"—Annette slumped next to her friend, shattered. A good girl through and through, she would never get used to this kind of attention, no matter how much of it she got— from studio executives, from her costars, from fans, from the world. Shy and insecure at her core, she was always sure she could be fired at any moment—in particular for growing out of her cute-little-Mouseketeer mold. "Annette freaked," Doreen says. "She absolutely freaked for weeks. She said, 'Oh my God, we're going to lose our jobs!'"

Not a chance. Whether she liked it or not, no one pleased every age bracket more than Annette, and none of the Mice would have more success doing so than she did. Viewers would watch the show every day *just* to see Annette say her name during Roll Call. Boys watching from home wished they could spend their whole day, not just an hour in the afternoon, watching their dream girl. Female

140

fans wanted to be just like Annette, but got a little miffed at how much the boys they knew talked about her. Unsubstantiated rumors that Annette was coming to someone's hometown for a visit could grind classes and Little League practices to a distracted halt. Her modest attitude about it all only made fans love her more.

Back at the beginning of the first season, a different girl had been on her way up the *Mickey Mouse Club* ladder. The gawkily pretty Darlene Gillespie—at fourteen, the oldest Mouse, beating Bobby by a month—had maturity, skill, and ambition. Her renditions of "When I Grow Up Someday" and "With a Smile and a Song" often forced tears from original director Dik Darley. "Darlene, to me, was the most talented by far," Bobby says, echoing a sentiment almost every other Mouseketeer shares.

When the fan mail started to pour in, though, the dynamic on set started to shift. The mail was a particular fixation for studio executives—the early TV industry had developed a rule of thumb, however unscientific, that every letter represented the feelings of about five hundred viewers. And thousands were telling them in no uncertain terms that it was Annette who was on her way to superstardom. "My son is six years old and has shown no noticeable desire for girls," one letter addressed to Annette said, "but he insists on seeing you daily." Another proclaimed: "Annette, in my book, you are beautiful. I dream of you every night." One fan spoke what was on the minds of many young boys: "There are a lot of girls in my class, but I don't think of them. I think of you."

Mouseketeers and fans alike could see what was happening—a star was being born before their eyes. "You stand on the sidelines and go, 'How come the camera loves Annette, and the most talented girl on this set is Darlene Gillespie?'" says dismissed first-season Mouse Paul Petersen, who watched Annette's meteoric rise and Darlene's surprising lack thereof from a fan's perspective. "And there's just no question about that. Darlene was pretty and could sing and could dance. But you can't do anything about the magical chemistry of a camera that makes Annette a star."

The young beauty's shyness translated onscreen as a sweet vulnerability that almost everyone seemed to adore. "The thing about Annette is not only did the guys like her, but the girls did too," says Sharon, one of Annette's lifelong best friends. Girls wished for dark, curly hair and big brown eyes like Annette's and they wanted to be ballerinas as graceful as she was. Doreen notes that the one talent for which Annette was not particularly famous, her dancing, was the one for which she deserved recognition: "In all honesty, she could have gone on to be a true ballerina. Physically, her body was strong, and she made it look like very little work. But she could do sixteen passés and you wouldn't even see the sweat. And I'm banging 'em away, trying to do 'em."

Male fans of the show were starting to feel, well, things they'd never felt before because of her. Her effect on boys was legendary: She melted them into quivering romantics. "You would like

Annette at once," Paul rhapsodizes in his memoir, "and probably forever." Don Agrati was among Annette's biggest fans when he joined the show in the third season, and he came to the set so infatuated with her that he could barely function around her at first. "My first line on the show was, 'Here they come, Annette!'" he recalls. "I was so nervous. And I so over-rehearsed the line: 'Here they come, *Annette!*' '*Here* they come, Annette!' 'Here *they* come, Annette!' When the time came to say it, I blew it. The director gave it to someone else. I was just crushed."

Annette was soon getting the vast majority of the show's letters—her mail alone accounted for six thousand envelopes per month at its peak. "Annette, you must have an awful lot of relatives back east," Walt once joked to the young starlet, "because you're getting more fan mail than anyone else." Some of her costars and their parents, eager for an explanation and worried for their own place in the show's hierarchy, repeated Walt's tease as truth to as many people as would listen. The idea that Annette's large Italian family was responsible for her perceived popularity would become one of the most persistent pieces of Mouskelore. "There was that theory that Annette's whole family just kept rewriting letters," Mary says. "But she was so talented and wonderful. Her talent was there, no doubt about it, no matter where the letters came from." Adds Doreen, "Annette would get so much fan mail, and it wasn't even planted. The American public always makes a breakout artist in any show. Annette was the breakout artist. You can't explain that at the time to a bunch of mothers, middle-class, frustrated about their own business. There was this 'I want my kid to be the best!' feeling."

Regardless of the source of her fan mail, it set Annette's career in motion as producers gave her more and more numbers and skits to anchor as she got more and more popular. Annette starred in her first serial in November 1956, "Adventure in Dairyland," the story of two actors who travel to Wisconsin to learn how to run a dairy farm. The new series worked well as Annette's transition to acting, since she was just playing herself. The onscreen family included a boy named Jimmy, who had a crush on Annette from watching her on *The Mickey Mouse Club*—a true-to-life situation if there ever was one.

Her momentum as a rising star just picked up from there. She also got a role in *The Further Adventures of Spin and Marty* as Spin's girlfriend, Annette, from the Circle H camp across the lake from the Triple R. She got her own ode, "Annette," from Jimmie Dodd, to which she performed a ballet solo in 1956. Annette cut-out dolls allowed fans to dress her in Mouseketeer gear, party dresses, or summer-picnic wear. When the second season of *The Mickey Mouse Club* hit, fans were surrounded by all things Annette.

As the Mice faced their viewers in person on publicity tours throughout the second season, it grew harder to ignore Annette's outsized popularity. Crowds would often chant her name. None of her costars said anything to her about it, but, she writes, "It made me feel self-conscious. I knew it wasn't my fault that I got more mail than the others; it was beyond my control. It did make me wish that audiences would scream just as loudly for all the others, and that perhaps I could melt back in as just one of twenty-four."

Annette grew increasingly uncomfortable with the disproportionate amount of attention directed her way. She was shy about signing more autographs than the other Mouseketeers, but didn't want to turn fans away, either. Press visiting the set would swarm her while ignoring her fellow Mice. Reporters writing about *The Mickey Mouse Club* recorded her awkwardness when she had to answer questions about her fame while other Mouseketeers were nearby. Annette would often deflect questions about herself by talking about her costars instead, but that modesty just fueled her fans' ardor.

Her costars couldn't always cover up their petty jealousy of her growing fame, and that sometimes erupted into squabbles. At one tour stop, "Uncle Makeup"—as the Mice called their makeup artist—thrilled the girls by letting them wear a little extra mascara. As Annette admired her luxurious, sophisticated—and still wet— lashes, another girl Mouse (she doesn't identify which one) came up behind her, put her hands right over Annette's eyes and sang, "Guess who!" The curtain went up seconds later, forcing Annette out onstage with her eyes a smudgy mess. "I was so mad," she writes, "but it all blew over, as those things seemed to do."

Darlene's competitive feelings toward Annette, however, had only just begun, according to her costars. "Darlene wasn't against

Annette as a person," Doreen says. "But she was very upset that everything went to Annette." Pressured by Annette's ever-eclipsing presence, Darlene agreed to spend the hiatus between the first and second seasons shooting Disney's *Westward Ho, the Wagons!* and cutting her first solo pop album for the company's fledgling record division. But Darlene, having pushed herself too much, contracted pneumonia and was forced to stay in bed for most of the hiatus while her film role in *Westward Ho* went to fellow Mouse Doreen, who happened to have the requisite horseback-riding skills.

As Darlene's ambition mounted in the second season, she started losing friends to the amiable Annette as well. Doreen, who'd befriended Darlene during the first season, started to distance herself from her talented onetime pal; Darlene may have inched away from Doreen also after her former friend grabbed the movie role meant for her. "I saw that there were problems with her," Doreen recalls. "She was working her butt off, trying to do everything just right." Doreen started spending most of her time with Annette and new girl Cheryl Holdridge instead, instigating troublemaking such as sneaking cigarettes from the hair and makeup room and smoking them in back corners of the soundstage.

Then Annette stumbled into a recording career, providing another reason for rivalry between Darlene and her. Darlene had been working overtime in the recording studio, singing the lead on a special-issue *Alice in Wonderland* album and becoming the first Mouse with her own LP-length record, *Darlene of the Teens*.

But then Annette got her own eponymous serial that was originally supposed to go to Darlene. It was based on the book *Margaret* by Janette Sebring Lowrey. Darlene was set to play the lead, a country girl who moves to the city, but producers then decided to give the role to Annette and name it after her to capitalize on her popularity. On one episode of the serial, Annette performed what she thought would be a onetime rendition of a song called "How Will I Know My Love." Sung during a hayride episode, this simple plea for guidance in recognizing the right boy for her struck a chord with viewers. Producers had at first considered having Annette lipsync to a more trained singer's voice, but at the last minute made the fateful decision to let her do it herself, despite what she calls her "three-note range." After it aired, thousands of fans wrote and called asking where to buy it on record.

Walt came to Annette and told her, "We've got to put this out on a single. We're getting fan letters like crazy. Kids want to buy it."

"I don't sing," Annette responded.

But Walt would have his way, of course. "Well, I'm signing you to a recording contract, young lady," he told her. "You're singing."

"Yes, sir," she answered, ever the dutiful Mouse (and under contract to do so).

And so it was that Annette became a pop star. She couldn't sing—as she had no trouble admitting—but that was no matter. "It was a wonderful experience until I heard the playback of my voice," she said in *Mouse Tracks: The Story of Walt Disney Records.* "*This is a disaster,* I thought to myself."

Producer Tutti Camarata knew his job was to make her sound good for the fans waiting to buy her single, so he walked her through the recording process. He set about trying to "fatten up" her voice, he explained in an interview, "as it was quite thin and hardly registered on the console meter. Echo alone did not seem to make enough of a difference and, after many experiments, I decided that we needed an overlay of a *second* Annette voice."

The solution finally came when a frustrated sound engineer switched on the high-end equalizer, saying, "Mr. Camarata, is this what you want?" And that's how "The Annette Sound" was created. Soon the song was out as a single. It sold several hundred thousand copies and spawned an entire album, *Songs from 'Annette' and Other Walt Disney Serials.* Annette would later credit the Disney echo chambers for her recording career, but that didn't stop her from becoming a full-fledged music force.

She'd go on to score a top-ten spot on the burgeoning rock 'n' roll charts with a cover of the song "Tall Paul," and she'd release several albums, including *Annette, Annette Sings Anka, Hawaiiannette,* and *Dance Annette.* The breakthrough success of her recording career took her outside the realm of the kid market before *The Mickey Mouse Club* even ended, and would later lead her to meet future screen love Frankie Avalon, once a mere doodle in her school binder, and real-life love Paul Anka. She was beginning the crossover from *The Mickey Mouse Club* to *American Bandstand* and beyond.

The Mickey Mouse Club cast in 1957, with lead Mooseketeer Jimmie Dodd. *Hulton Archive/Getty Images*

Walt Disney, upon signing his historic 1954 TV production agreement with ABC, which would lead first to the *Disneyland* anthology series and, a year later, *The Mickey Mouse Club*.
Bettmann/Corbis

Lonnie Burr in his first-year Mouse ears. He has his pompadour wave pushed out in front in defiance of producers' wishes that he and the other boys wear their hats straight across their foreheads.
Courtesy of Lonnie Burr

Breakout Mouseketeer
Annette Funicello and
adult host Jimmie Dodd
in a 1957 promotional
shot, complete with
Mouse Club guitar.
Hulton Archive/Getty Images

Jimmie Dodd and Roy Williams,
the two grown-up "Mooseketeers."
Jimmie was known for his
Christian-based morality lessons,
called "Doddisms," and for writing
the "Mickey Mouse Club March."
Roy was known for his bawdy
sense of humor and for conceiving
the iconic Mouse ears.
Hulton Archive/Getty Images

"Unknown Mouseketeer" Dallas Johann, who was released from his contract before the show even aired because he cried whenever the camera was on him. Sadly, he didn't get to keep his Mouse ears either.
Courtesy of Dallas Johann

Tim Considine, known to *Mouse Club* fans as the star of the popular serial *The Adventures of Spin and Marty*, in which he played cocky ranch-hand Spin Evans.
ABC Photo Archives/Getty Images

Adventures of Spin and Marty star David Stollery in one of his earlier roles, with Victor Moore in the Broadway play *On Borrowed Time. Mouse Club* viewers knew him as snooty Martin Markham.
Yale Joel/Time Life Pictures/Getty Images

Second-season Mouseketeer Eileen Diamond, posing in the yard in her new *Mouse Club* uniform. *Courtesy of Eileen Rogosin (née Diamond)*

Third-season addition Don Agrati (who'd later change his last name to Grady), performing in his pre-Mouseketeer days in the San Francisco Bay area. *Courtesy of Don Grady*

Annette Funicello and Darlene Gillespie guest-starred together in the third installment of the popular *Spin and Marty* serials, playing girls at a neighboring ranch camp. *ABC Photo Archives/Getty Images*

Annette Funicello at the peak of her Mouseketeer stardom, readying for a scene in her self-titled serial *Annette*. Notoriously boy-crazy, she lined her dressing room mirror with photos of her star crush, *Zorro*'s Guy Williams. *ABC Photo Archives/Getty Images*

Walt Disney greets Mouseketeers as they arrive at Disneyland in 1955, shortly after the show's debut that October. *Metro Library and Archive*

Christening the Disneyland bus. Mouseketeers were constantly on call to appear at any promotional events Disney deemed necessary, even on weekends, which made for an overwhelming schedule. *Metro Library and Archive*

The Mickey Mouse Club's three biggest heartthrobs: *Spin and Marty's* David Stollery and (blocked by a fan) Tim Considine flank Annette Funicello as they sign autographs at Disneyland. *Charles Phoenix collection*

Mouseketeers visit Melbourne, Australia, in 1959, in a tour appearance sponsored by the State Savings Bank of Victoria. Even though the *Club* had been canceled in America, its stars got to revel in their peaking popularity Down Under. "There were more people to greet us there than Frank Sinatra when he arrived," Mouseketeer Sharon Baird said. "I thought that was really something." *Public Record Office Victoria*

Two *Mouse Club* graduates
found greater fame on the long-
running family sitcom My *Three
Sons*: Don Grady, left, as middle
brother Robbie Douglas, and
Tim Considine, right, as oldest
Mike. *Bettmann/Corbis*

Don Grady playing bass
at the peak of his teen-
idol status, in the mid-
sixties. After My *Three
Sons*, he would segue into
a music career. *Courtesy of
Don Grady*

Annette Funicello and Frankie Avalon play to the camera in a scene from their memorable 1963 movie *Beach Party*. She kept her navel covered, just as her mentor Walt Disney had requested. *Bettmann/Corbis*

Annette Funicello plays with the Beach Boys in *The Monkey's Uncle* as she shoots to post–*Mickey Mouse Club* superstardom. *RB/Redferns*

Mouseketeer beauties and lifelong best friends Doreen Tracey and Cheryl Holdridge in the 1960s. *Courtesy of Doreen Tracey*

"Unknown Mouseketeer" Dallas Johann makes peace with Mickey Mouse as an adult, years after leaving the show before it even aired because of camera fright. *Courtesy of Dallas Johann*

Lonnie Burr performing at the Mousketeers' twenty-fifth anniversary party at Disneyland in 1980. His Mouse ears from that performance would later be on display at the Smithsonian. *Courtesy of Lonnie Burr*

Annette Funicello, Judy Harriet, and Eileen Rogosin (née Diamond) pose with their children at the 1980 reunion. *Courtesy of Eileen Rogosin*

Annette Funicello cements her Disney-legend status in 1997 as Disney CEO Michael Eisner looks on, along with Mickey and Minnie. *Time & Love Pictures/Getty Images*

Cheryl Holdridge, Doreen Tracey, Bobby Burgess, and Tommy Cole attend the Hollywood Collectors & Celebrities Show in North Hollywood in 2001. The Mouseketeers have become a happy fixture at autograph conventions. *Getty Images*

Tommy Cole with a framed cast photo in his Los Angeles area home. The Mouseketeers' resident male crooner left performing behind in favor of a long-running career behind-the-scenes in makeup artistry. *Courtesy of the author*

Sharon Baird in her room, full of Mickey Mouse paraphernalia. After a fruitful run of playing costumed characters on TV shows such as *Land of the Lost* and *The New Zoo Revue*, she retired to Reno, Nevada. *Courtesy of the author*

David Stollery outside his Orange County, California, office with his prized AREX sportscar, his own creation. He quit show business right after *Spin and Marty* ended to follow his real passion, designing cars. *Courtesy of the author*

Actor-turned-writer Tim Considine in his book-lined Southern California office. He specializes in automotive writing and has penned several articles about his *Spin and Marty* costar. *Courtesy of the author*

Sherry Van Meter (a.k.a. Sherry Allen) performs at the Mouseketeers' fiftieth reunion. *Courtesy of Sherry Van Meter*

"I didn't even want to go to Disneyland," Mary Espinosa Goff said of the years after being dismissed from the show. "I felt like I was a failure because I got dropped." She eventually came to terms with her feelings of rejection and had a ball at the fiftieth *Mouse Club* reunion. She's shown smiling here, second from left, with costars Bobby Burgess, Doreen Tracey, Sharon Baird, Sherry Van Meter (a.k.a. Sherry Allen), and Cheryl Holdridge. *Courtesy of Mary Espinosa Goff*

Cheryl Holdridge and Doreen Tracey celebrate fifty years of post-*Mouse Club* friendship. This 2005 shot would be their last together; Cheryl died of cancer in January 2009. *Courtesy of Doreen Tracey*

Mouseketeers perform with Mickey at their fiftieth-anniversary celebration. Annette could no longer join in the festivities because of her protracted battle with multiple sclerosis, but the rest gamely donned the Mouse ears once more. "It bothers me that we still have to wear them," Karen Pendleton said. "But at least they make them fancy and put glitter on them now." *Courtesy of Sherry Van Meter*

*   *   *

Now Annette had managed to upstage Darlene even in the music business, of all things—the one area where Darlene had an unmistakable natural advantage. Darlene could make producers cry with her live voice, and had wowed critics with her *Darlene of the Teens* album; but here Annette was becoming a huge star with the help of echo chambers and multiple recordings of her voice layered on top of each other. Worse still, the project that could have been Darlene's first clear triumph—playing the lead in a planned Disney theatrical release, *The Rainbow Road to Oz*—would become yet another doomed endeavor. At first, Disney had so much confidence in the movie, despite not having seen a full script yet, that the Mice appeared on *Disneyland*'s fourth-anniversary episode in September 1957 to preview two scenes from it. But the script didn't meet Walt's standards, and the *Oz* project was canceled by May 1958.

Burned by continued disappointment, Darlene and her father, her costars say, grew obsessed with Annette's stardom and Darlene's perceived lack thereof. "Annie was especially feeling duress because by now Darlene and her father were consumed by Annie's success and Darlene's sputtering trip to nowhere despite having her own series and making solo records and albums, and they both took it out on Annie more than previously," Lonnie says in his memoir. "Annie said they were constantly berating her verbally and they were very cruel."

The rest of the Mouseketeers swear Annette's fame didn't stoke their own jealousies, but say they understood why Darlene may have felt that way. "I never thought anyone felt any competition with Annette *except* Darlene," Cubby says. "She felt basically betrayed by Disney. He promised to make *her* a star and *Annette* became a star. I don't know if that even really happened or not, but that was how she felt." Adds Tommy, "Darlene was very popular also, but Annie was doted on by Walt, because Walt's the one who discovered her." Darlene grew ever more "glamorized," as Bobby says, dying her dishwater hair blonder and gluing on painstaking false eyelashes. "She was competing with Annette, and she couldn't," he says. "Annette was such a natural."

Darlene later blamed the conflict on the producers: "I think all those stories about jealousy between Annette and me were largely caused by adults," she told author Jerry Bowles in his 1976 book, *Forever Hold Your Banner High!* "Somehow, they tried to make everything competitive, which is a monstrous thing to do to a kid. No wonder kids who get into show business early often have tremendous adjustment problems when they get older. Christ, it's enough to warp your whole value system. Somehow, you are made to think that winning is more important than being a good human being." It seemed, though, she never quite got over feeling she wasn't winning, "The real reason I never liked Annette," she added later in the interview, "is because she always got the new tap shoes. I had to wear the same godddamned shoes until I was eighteen. It nearly crippled me for life."

Annette's other would-be rivals loved her too much to be jealous, and tend, if anything, to defend their Annie. They like nothing more than to talk about her unassailable charm: "She was always so sweet to me," Karen says. "Annette was sixteen and I was like twelve toward the end of the show, but she never ignored me." First love Lonnie takes particular pride in spotting her star quality before most of the other boys in the world: "I believe that I inferred something about this lady before anyone else except maybe Walt," he writes. "Despite her success as a child and adult acting star and vocalist, Annie always maintained that she was not the best actor, not the best singer, not the best dancer. She was talented, of course, but she is honest and correct in that assessment. What she has always been is *charismatic*." Adds Tommy, "We all loved her, Annie. She's just one of those special people who stayed the same throughout her fame."

As Annette's fame continued to grow, however, *The Mickey Mouse Club* was headed in the other direction. Despite producers' continued efforts to freshen up the cast, the awkward adolescence of the core group of Mice, the aging of their fans, and the disproportionate popularity of Annette was throwing the onetime hit off balance and sending it down the ratings charts. The question became only a matter of when, not whether, the show would end. And what would become of the Mice when it did.

151

Part 3

THE AFTERMATH

Chapter Ten

The End of the Club

The Mouseketeers crowded onto their stage, just as they had done hundreds of times throughout their three years on the air. "Okay, now you're seeing something happy, and it makes you laugh," director Sid Miller instructed them. They delivered their specialty: the loudest, happiest cheer with the biggest, happiest grins possible on their faces.

Then Miller yelled, "Cut!" and everything changed. The minute the cameras stopped and the all-clear bell rang, the Mice slumped and sighed. Their faces quivered with held-back sobs. Many actually broke into tears. Though they were shooting the standard gleeful reaction shots for Circus Day, something they'd done often in their time as Mouseketeers, this time was different. It was the official last take of the last scene they would ever shoot during their time on *The Mickey Mouse Club*.

"You'd see us on camera going, 'Yaaaay!'" Sharon recalls. "And then as soon as we finished we were just, 'Uhhhh.' It was just, chills." As soon as it ended, Annette and Sharon shared a box of

Kleenex. The two brought autograph books to the set that day, which they made everyone sign, yearbook-style. The Mouskemoms joined in the sniffling too. "It's a very dramatic stage," Sharon says. "We're dramatic to start with and then to be in your teens like that and to be that close…" Adds Cubby, "We were all sad. I think mostly we were sad that we weren't going to see each other and that different things were going to happen now." But some of the older boys felt less sentimental. Lonnie Burr was downright happy to finally be set free: "I felt it was too childish, puerile, unsophisticated for me," he says. "I'm trying to be Cary Grant, as I'm getting older in my teens. I wouldn't watch this show if I could!" Bobby, on the other hand, hated to say good-bye, but the seventeen-year-old was excited to get on with his life. "The guys were ready to see what was out there," he says. "I was sad because I liked the steadiness of it, but I mostly watched the girls cry."

Miller stifled his crankier tendencies to give his charges some words of wisdom: "Don't cry, because the more you work in this business, the more you'll be working together again."

Tears were in order, though. As the third season came to an end in 1958, the producers had dropped the bad news on the kids. This time, it wasn't just *some* of the Mice being fired. It was all of them. *The Mickey Mouse Club*'s massive popularity could not be sustained at the dizzying levels it had reached, and its biggest idols—Annette Funicello and the *Spin and Marty* boys—were outgrowing their audience with no prospect of new breakout heartthrobs in the cast to take their place in America's hearts.

Just like that, the Mouseketeers would go from spending all of their time together to none. They would lose their home for the past three years, Sound Stage 1, and their second family, the Mouseketeers. "It seemed to me and to some of the other kids that a wonderful part of our lives was being wrenched away," Annette writes. "And there was nothing anyone could do about it. This was without a doubt the greatest disappointment of my young life."

A cloud of angst hung over their waning days on set. "Why are they canceling our show?" they asked one another. "It's so popular." "I can't believe it! How can they do this?" For all they knew, they'd never see one another again. And what would they do now, day after day? Would they go back to regular school to be mocked? Would they ever feel the thrill of dancing and singing before an audience of millions again? And the biggest question of all: How had this happened to their show?

Though the series had become a fixture in pop culture, refrains of "The Mouse got killed"—TV-business parlance for the Club not doing so hot in the ratings—echoed more frequently throughout ABC's network offices. Ratings were slipping from their peak of four-teen million viewers down toward the ten-million mark. The cost to produce the show was starting to outweigh its benefits, ABC said. As network president Robert Kintner—the man who'd just a few years earlier predicted that the show would have "the greatest impact on children in the history of television"—now said, "There are only a certain number of sponsors that will sponsor a so-called kid show, and they have only a certain amount in their budgets." Walt Disney groused that ABC was killing the show with too many commercial breaks, but there was no denying that, as *Variety* posited, "the novelty of *Mickey Mouse* may have worn off." *American Bandstand*, the Club's lead-in from four to five p.m., was fast surpassing the one-time phenomenon of the Mouseketeers in cool factor, catering to the exact older-teen audience *The Mickey Mouse Club* was losing.

Perhaps more important, ABC wanted out of the Disneyland deal it had made to get *Disneyland* and *The Mickey Mouse Club*. "I thought it was time we reevaluated our whole relationship with Disney," network chairman Leonard Goldenson writes. "The only reason we'd taken a position in Disneyland was to get them into television, but the Disneys had turned out to be terrible business partners. Disneyland had become enormously successful, but Disney kept plowing his profits back into park expansion. I feared that it would be a very long time before we started seeing any return on our original $500,000 investment." Walt Disney had soured on the relationship as well: "What did they do to help build the place?" he complained of ABC's stake in his dream park.

Soon, ABC and Disney saw the writing on the wall. It took some complicated legal wrangling—including a court battle over whether Disney could try to sell *The Mickey Mouse Club* to another network—but after 360 shows, it really was time to say good-bye, for good.

Because the cachet of being a Mouseketeer was no longer what it once was just a year earlier, it remained to be seen which of the Mouseketeers would be working again in Hollywood—and which of them would go the way of so many child stars, right back into an intolerable kind of obscurity. Annette's future was the only one that was clear; in fact, her path was already settled before that last day of filming. A few weeks earlier, a Disney executive had pulled her and her mother aside for a talk. Annette had panicked, thinking the day had at last come: She was getting fired for being too tall. Instead, the Funicellos got the news that Disney wanted to keep Annette—Walt Disney's single greatest contribution to *The Mickey Mouse Club*—under contract with the studio after the show ended. She carried the awkward secret with her even as her costars wept around her and wondered about their own futures.

As it turned out, she would become the only Mouse to stick around. The rest were cut loose without another word from the studio, except for Cubby and Karen, who declined a joint contract offer. Cubby was already moving on to other ventures, though Karen would wish for years to come that she and her parents had thought to at least ask Disney to consider her as a solo act: "I can't imagine how my life would've been different if I'd done it," she says. Like most of her costars, she had no idea how hard it would be to continue the showbiz career she'd started so easily on *The Mickey Mouse Club*. But as they'd all learn eventually, not all former Mouseketeers were created equal.

The months immediately following the show's end disappointed many a Mouse. "Once the show was over and you went out on auditions," Sharon says, "people didn't want you because you were stereotyped." Adds Tommy, "I was in that transitional period as an actor. Here I'm off a hit show and I'm a singer-dancer. But nobody wanted to hire us. They didn't even consider us actors, not knowing, not realizing, that all we were doing was acting on the show. We always had lines we memorized. And the music and dancing and putting everything together should be a lot harder than just being an actor."

But then Jimmie Dodd stepped in to rescue them from all that—for at least a few weeks. Jimmie took up the mantle to keep *The Mickey Mouse Club* alive with a performance tour to Sydney, Australia, in 1959. He agreed to lead his former costars to visit their growing fan base Down Under, prolonging the Mouseketeers' days of fame—and, in fact, giving them a way to live out an even more heightened version of what they'd experienced at the pinnacle of their U.S. celebrity.

When the ex-Mouseketeers' plane touched down in Sydney, they found thousands of fans had crammed the airport to greet them. When Jimmie, Sharon, Doreen, Bobby, Cubby, Karen, and Tommy stepped off the plane on the tarmac, the crowd broke through the ropes in a rush to get closer to their idols. Airport security hurried the stars back onto their jet, then came up with a safer way to get them to the gate: by rolling them as they stood on the movable stairs normally used to get off the plane, whisking them by their adoring public.

Jimmie led his charges out through the airport, with all of them scurrying past the overwhelming crowd behind their leader. All except Doreen, that is, who, in her seventeen-year-old, tight-pink-T-shirted glory took in every last bit of slack-jawed adulation. "I *loved* it," she says. "And I *was* loved."

From the second they arrived, the Mice would get their own personal bodyguards. The security team had to resort to extreme measures at times to get the teens to their limos in one piece before the delirious fans would start rocking their cars back and forth, trying to get a glimpse of the famous faces inside. "There were more people to greet us there than Frank Sinatra when he arrived," Sharon marvels. "I thought that was really something."

Fans lined the streets from the airport to the Rex Hotel, where the ex-Mice were staying, just to wave as they passed. Crowds waited outside the hotel hoping for autographs. "The Rex Hotel had to close the streets because there were just throngs of people around the hotel chanting our names," Tommy marvels. "When we went to sign autographs, they'd have to cut it off because we'd be signing twenty-four hours a day [if we accommodated everyone]." Concert audiences clamored for them. Karen remained mystified that she, of all people, could be such a huge star to anyone. "The crowd was pounding their feet," she says, "and I remember thinking I had no idea why." Adds Bobby, "That's when I really felt famous, with thousands of people waiting at the airport for us."

The Mickey Mouse Club had just started airing on Aussie TV, and it was a huge hit—it would run in syndication there for more than a decade. So the trip had the surreal effect of resurrecting the Club alumni's fame right before their eyes, exactly when they needed it, and exactly at the age when they could enjoy it. When they'd first become famous a few years earlier Stateside, they'd been sweating through constant rehearsals and tapings while locked inside the Disney studio walls, too busy to appreciate their celebrity. Now reminders of their popularity surrounded them, swarmed them, just when they were full-fledged teenagers thirsty for an ego boost and a good time.

The Australia outing allowed the ex-Mice to escape the fruitless auditions and the dreary school life they'd been thrust back into and trade it for a fan base who idolized them overseas. Tommy would, in fact, return for several more Australian appearances, doing variety shows, playing clubs, and touring with pop singer Jimmie Rodgers, always seeking the fame he couldn't find back home. "I should have stayed there, because I was a big name there," he says. "But then I came back and couldn't buy a job."

Doreen recognized the tour as exactly what she'd been waiting for. She enjoyed the Australia trip like no one else. She kicked things off by teaching Cubby, now thirteen, how to French kiss on the plane during the fourteen-hour flight to Sydney. "I learned a lot from nine years old to fourteen," Cubby says, with much of the credit going to the budding bombshell. Memorable for Cubby, but just another boring day for Doreen during this trip. "I was sixteen years old, I had flaming red hair, and Britney Spears had nothing on me," she says. True enough, she'd come to the continent with more curves than ever, and a mischievous, pin-up-girl look that could only lead to trouble. The trip marked the first time Doreen didn't have to compete for attention with either the dreamy Annette—whom the studio wouldn't free from her movie commitments for the trip—or the songbird Darlene Gillespie—who declined an invitation to go. Doreen took it all, happily.

Australian newspapers charted her every "sexpot" move, including her liaison with Dave Somerville, the perfectly coiffed lead singer of Canadian quartet the Diamonds, who opened for the Mouseketeers on the tour. "He looked like Tony Curtis, and I was dying," she recalls. "So I used to be in the bar downstairs drinking Pimms with him after the shows. He was twenty-five and I was seventeen. I was a very bad girl." Doreen's mother broke the affair up, as she didn't like reading about her daughter's love life with her morning coffee, particularly when it involved cavorting with a twenty-something rock 'n' roll star. Doreen continued to sneak out with the older man anyway until the trip was over.

The memories of the tour would stick with them like no others from their time as Mouseketeers. "Before then, I don't think I realized how big the show was," Sharon says. "And I would never forget how that felt."

When they got back home, things were far different. While *The Mickey Mouse Club*'s newfound popularity in Australia made for glamorous tours, the show's surprising second life in America made life worse instead of better for the former Mice. A fourth season consisting of reruns and repackagings of the first two seasons ran in 1959, mocking its stars with younger versions of themselves just as they tried to transition into the vicious "real world" of school and peers. They'd return to the airwaves yet again, in syndication running from 1962 to 1965. The show that had allegedly run out of steam now refused to die, even as its stars tried to make post-Mouse lives for themselves.

The clash between the Mouseketeers' former selves still on television and the teenagers careening toward adulthood who they now were highlighted the larger conflict that would mar their lives for years to come: the idyllic '50s sensibility their screen images represented versus the hipper grown-ups they were trying to become. "After a while it was a part of my life that I wanted over, and it just wouldn't die," Dennis Day said in an interview. "There were all those reruns, and people kept recognizing me."

This conflict first played itself out in the halls of the schools to which the Mouseketeers were hoping to return quietly and without incident. Kids in Karen's seventh-grade class would ask her for her autograph, but when the guileless middle-schooler would give it to them, they'd tear it up in front of her. "What a time to go back to school," she says. "There were so many kids who were mean to me. They'd gather around me at lunchtime, and the vice principal would have to come and get me out. It did no wonders for my self-esteem, which was already low anyway." Her classmates would say things like, "Wiggle your ears and I'll give you some cheese." Some boys threw a worm at her. All she could do was wait for the novelty of torturing a former Mouseketeer to wear off, which would take longer than she'd hoped: "Even through high school and a couple of times in college, people would still say things to me. And dating was hard. It was hard to do, to be attached to a Mouse."

Don Agrati, a tiny thirteen-year-old, acquired the nickname "Mouse" the second he returned to public school and suffered from the same unoriginal—though still hurtful—teasing methods his first love, Karen, was also enduring. Kids would sing "The Mickey Mouse Club March" whenever he entered the cafeteria. "I was in fights every day and I was just miserable," he recalls. "So my parents took me out of the school. They said, 'You know what, you need to start over again. And the same thing's going to happen. You have to respond, react differently this time.' The same thing, the exact same thing, happened the first day I was at the cafeteria in the new school. I walked in, they started singing the *Mickey Mouse Club* song. But this time I just joined in. And it worked. That was it. I just needed to do that once and it was like they saw that I was fun and it was over."

Tommy Cole had to switch schools too because of his ex-Mouseketeer status. His hometown school wasn't forgiving of the classwork he'd missed while on *The Mickey Mouse Club*, even though he'd been attending to his studies in the studio-lot trailers as required by law. He tried to return to John Muir High School in Pasadena, but he couldn't catch a break. "John Muir had no idea what a show kid was, none whatsoever," he recalls. "They did not give me a bit of slack on anything. They gave me a real hard time, and my parents finally pulled me out of there. I finished up my high school at Hollywood Professional School because they understand showbiz there."

Doreen Tracey went straight to Hollywood Professional upon returning from Australia, sure she'd need a school that would cut her extra slack for the huge career she was convinced she'd have after her intoxicating time Down Under. "My ego was sooo big," she says. "Then…nothing. Not even an interview. My agent didn't send me out for six months." And the memories of cheering fans and older rock 'n' roll stars romancing her in Australia couldn't get her out of having to finish classes at the "dive way down on Hollywood Boulevard," as she calls the school that Tommy, Cubby, and Lonnie now also attended. She liked that the school understood the rigors of show-business life: Whether you were off shooting a movie or simply indulging your child-star rebellion, "you'd just get a slap on the hand and a C," Doreen explains. But soon, her friend and classmate Barbara Parkins, a glamorous brunette who'd go on to star in *Valley of the Dolls*, encouraged Doreen to transfer to Hollywood High with her for its better academic reputation, so she did.

Right after they switched schools, though, Doreen found herself on the outs with Barbara, and as a new girl at the school, Doreen says she "was not accepted into the club. So now I'm a total outcast." She rethought her master plan yet again, deciding to focus this time on teaching classes at her father's studio after school. "I thought, I'm going to clean up my act and be a ballet girl and just cool it. Just get my grades up because I really wanted to go to either Yale or Harvard. I had interviews with a couple of the counselors that thought

I could get in on my celebrity. So I had to buckle down and get my grades." Then, however, another surprise: "I fell in love. Married my high school sweetheart. His name was Robert Washburn. I graduated high school. Had a baby." In an exclusive *Teen Magazine* interview in 1962, Doreen said she and Bob had their wedding on May 7, 1961, just after she'd turned eighteen, only to reveal in a later interview that they'd eloped to Tijuana months earlier. In any case, she had her son by early 1962 and divorced by fall 1963.

Only Bobby managed a smooth transition from *The Mickey Mouse Club* to regular school, perhaps because he returned home to his parents' place in Long Beach, thirty-seven long miles from Walt Disney Studios. "My mother and dad never moved, because they didn't want me to be real showbizzy," he says. Sure, the kids back at Long Beach Polytechnic High called him "Mickey" throughout his senior year, but he wasn't the kind of guy who took much offense at that. Then he went on to Cal State Long Beach while dating his first dance partner, Barbara Boylan, whom he'd met when he was twelve and once grooved with in a routine for *The Mickey Mouse Club*'s Talent Round-Up. He studied drama and became a Sigma Pi. "I got in a fraternity 'cause I wanted to pretty much get back to normal. I made lifetime friends, and we still get together."

Meanwhile, the official end of *The Mickey Mouse Club* liberated David Stollery in a way he hadn't realized he wanted. "Acting, for me, was a job," he says, "something I had to do and didn't have a choice. I just did it, as well as I could and correctly. But when I had the choice, I went, 'Okay, *this* is what I want instead.'"

After spending most of his young life in front of cameras and on stages—and having the savings account to prove it—he didn't have to ask his parents for college money. He told them he'd be attending the Art Center College of Design in Pasadena. He'd always known, since those days of playing toy cars with Tim and drawing impromptu sketches of houses for future Cubby and Karen to live in: He wanted a career in design, particularly in the automotive industry. "I was just like, 'I want to be a designer. I'm going to go to that school.' You know, I had the money."

Many of the Mouseketeers were finding it hard to fit into the world outside the Disney bubble, but there was no going back to the Magic Kingdom, either—a harsh realization Tommy faced when he returned to Disney Studios to visit one day, three years after *The Mickey Mouse Club* stopped shooting.

As soon as he set foot inside the lot, he had that surreal feeling you get when you visit an old school, like you're seeing a place from a dream you once had, like you're a little surprised to find life there still moving forward without you. He hadn't been to the studio much since he and the rest of the Mouseketeers had shot their final *Mickey Mouse Club* episode. Tommy and the rest of the ex-Mouseketeers not named Annette Funicello had found little reason to visit the lot in the intervening years, except for those few Australia tour rehearsals. "But I came to visit Gertie, who was the wardrobe person from *The Mickey Mouse Club*, because we'd become friends," he says. "Every now and again I'd say hi to her."

The nineteen-year-old boy, who had yet to figure out his place in Hollywood, had always loved the crew who made the complicated mess of *The Mickey Mouse Club* run so smoothly every day. When he was walking over to find Gertie, however, a guard he knew, a guy named John, stopped him near where a shoot was going on for a new Disney musical, *Babes in Toyland*, which starred none other than Annette. "Do not go on the set," the guard told him. "It's a closed set."

"Okay, John," Tommy answered. "I won't."

But after John walked away, just as Tommy passed by the stage door, out came eighteen-year-old Annie, in all her smooth-coiffed, mascara-coated, Annette Funicello–ness. "Tommy!" she squealed, running to hug him. "Come on in and watch the shoot!"

"Well," he demurred, "I was told not to go on the set."

"Oh, but you're my guest," she said. "Come on."

"I went in and watched for a while," he says. But as soon as Annette flitted back into the haze of cameras and crew and makeup and wardrobe to do her job, Tommy felt a tap on his shoulder. His stomach plummeted. There stood guard John, the human embodiment of how things had changed since the last time Tommy had been on a set with Annie. John motioned for Tommy to leave. Like a good Mouseketeer, Tommy obeyed.

"It was just an isolated incident, but it was kind of ironic," Tommy says now. "Here I was now, persona non grata."

The contrast between Annette's post–*Mickey Mouse Club* career and those of many of her costars couldn't be denied. While many ex-Mice gave up on Hollywood in frustration, a year after *The Mickey Mouse Club* ended, Annette had become even more popular than she'd been at the height of her Mouseketeerdom. In January 1959, Disneyland Records released "Tall Paul," her first top-10 hit. She appeared on several episodes of *Disneyland* and shot a guest role on Danny Thomas's *Make Room for Daddy* in March of 1959, the same month her star turn in Disney's *The Shaggy Dog* hit the big screen. There was no escaping the most famous former Mouse in the spring of 1959.

However, even golden-girl Annette's transition from Mouse to movie star proved bumpier than expected. She quietly filed a lawsuit in December of 1959 to break her seven-year Disney contract that began with *The Mickey Mouse Club*'s first season in 1955, arguing that her deal was unfair because she'd had neither an agent nor a lawyer at the time she signed it. More to the point, she'd become a much bigger star than expected. The seventeen-year-old—who was now making just $325 per week despite her pop-chart domination and box-office draw—lost her first attempt, but sued again the following year and won an increase in pay to $500 a week, with scheduled increases topping out at $1,050 a week over the next four years.

The case played out as a rather civil business affair once she got her due, and she stayed comfortably with Disney for a few more years. Soon she was shooting *Babes in Toyland,* as well as *The*

Misadventures of Merlin Jones and *The Monkey's Uncle,* for Walt Disney Pictures. She never mentions the suit in her 1995 autobiography, *A Dream Is a Wish Your Heart Makes,* and she's remained loyal to Walt throughout her lifetime, never missing a chance to attribute her success to "Mr. Disney."

A few other Club stars, however, were finding there was life—and even stardom—well outside Mr. Disney's sprawling Magic Kingdom domain. *My Three Sons,* for instance, emerged as a happy haven for ex-Mice: In 1960 Tim Considine became the eldest of Fred MacMurray's titular offspring on the ABC sitcom. Little Don Agrati—who had, since *The Mickey Mouse Club,* gotten himself a few roles as "the dramatic kid in the Western who was protecting his mother from his alcoholic father," as he says—landed himself the part of Tim's younger brother on *My Three Sons.*

Both boys would become bigger teen idols on *Sons* than they had on the *Mouse Club*—particularly Don, who'd been too young and had become a Mouseketeer too late to gain much momentum. Now going by the stage name Don Grady, he graced *Teen Magazine* covers all by himself, making grand pronouncements like, "I don't want to be an idol!" Tim had declared himself retired post–*Mickey Mouse Club*—the second of several retirements from Hollywood for the heartthrob—but his agent talked him back onscreen and into what would become one of the most successful classic family television series. Sherry and Cheryl would both snag a few guest spots on the show, as well, playing a different girl each time—a common '50s TV practice. "I was on the show four or five times,"

Sherry says. "I played Don Grady's girlfriend, I played Barry Livingston's girlfriend...I played everybody's girlfriend on that show."

My Three Sons also offered an unexpected career boost to Tommy as he searched for his place in showbiz post-Mouseketeerdom. His mom, inspired by her years of sitting with the other mothers on the Disney lot, fashioned a small business out of being the on-set guardian for child actors whose parents worked. While she was "sitting" for sixteen-year-old Don on *Sons*, Tommy would often tag along. That won him parts on a few episodes, but more important, Tommy, always more interested in the crew than the cast, struck up a friendship with a makeup artist on set who ended up inspiring Tommy's entire life's work. "I got interested because he said back then that makeup was one of the highest-paid positions on the set," Tommy says. "You never got your hands dirty from pulling cable. You wore a tie, you always were respected. Makeup is the necessary evil on the set. I just fell into it. I didn't want to be a singer in a bar in my fifties in some sleazy club. My living would be working with pretty actresses now instead."

The Lawrence Welk Show proved another easy transitional route for former Mouseketeers. Cubby found work on the hit variety show right away—without his onscreen other half, Karen. Having turned down the ongoing deal with Disney, the drumming prodigy, now twelve, auditioned for a gig on *Lawrence Welk* just after *The Mickey Mouse Club*'s final taping. ABC's popular variety hour was looking to add a "junior band" to its mix of ballroom dancers and orchestral performances. The kids would play for half of the Wednesday-night broadcast. The little drummer got the job, though the kiddie band idea lasted only six months. Welk asked Cubby to stay on and play with the adult band afterward, which he did for two years, a job that prepared him for the rigors of live performance. At the Hollywood Professional School, he put together his own band and also worked up a bit of a club act with Sherry, whom he dated for a while. "At that time there were lounges in every Holiday Inn, so we played there," he remembers. "She was a hot number." He did some acting as well, appearing in Western series such as *Zane Grey Theater* and *Cheyenne*. "But I always felt more comfortable as a musician," he says. "It was really my thing."

Just around the time Cubby left *The Lawrence Welk Show*, Bobby joined it. While a student at Cal State, he entered a contest with dance partner/girlfriend Barbara Boylan, aiming to win a chance to appear on *Welk*. They wowed viewers so much they'd dance together on the show for the next six years. Bobby would stick around for the show's entire run, until 1982, and would never get around to finishing his degree—he's still nine units short. But that didn't stop his fraternity brothers from supporting him all the way. "When I was on the show, they'd come and see it and they'd scream and yell," he says, "which Lawrence really loved." He'd almost always perform his own choreography—including several routines that were just slight variations on numbers from his *Mickey Mouse Club* days. He often notes that "*Lawrence Welk* is kind of an adult *Mickey Mouse Club*." And that was exactly why he liked it.

Cheryl went the TV route to fame at first as well, finding success thanks to roles on *Leave It to Beaver* and *The Rifleman*. But she achieved a gossip-column level of notoriety in 1964 when she married Woolworth department store heir Lance Reventlow in a glitzy Los Angeles ceremony. The rich playboy and the twenty-year-old tomboy—they got along because she knew her cars—wed in front of six hundred guests oozing Hollywood glamour at the Westwood Community Methodist Church. Cary Grant and Dyan Cannon stood among the crowd, all of whom were so rapt they forgot to sit down as the Barbie blonde and the car-racing daredevil said their vows. Doreen Tracey smiled up at the front of the church next to the couple in her hot pink maid of honor's dress (and a brunette wig, as she was blond at the time and Cheryl didn't want their hair to match). It was, as Doreen called it, "a real Cecil B. DeMille production. She did okay for herself. *Very* okay."

As a bittersweet result of her wedding, however, Cheryl would be the last Mouseketeer to ever see their beloved Mooseketeer Jimmie Dodd alive. When the newly pronounced Mr. and Mrs. Lance Reventlow jetted off to Hawaii for their month-long honeymoon, their first stop on Oahu was the Queen's Hospital in Honolulu, where Jimmie had lain ill for three months. After those two Australia tours plus a few intervening years of occasional Disney-related appearances, the ex-Mooseketeer had moved with his wife, Ruth, to Hawaii in the summer of 1964 to put together a local children's television show to be called *Jimmie Dodd's Aloha Time*. They shot for just one day before Dodd landed in the hospital with a staph infection and never left.

When Cheryl and Lance tiptoed into his room as newlyweds,

Jimmie was asleep. They left him a note, then snuck back out as quietly as they had arrived. Jimmie died the next day, November 10, at the age of fifty-four. Though Cheryl would later bring her new husband to dinner with Roy, she said one of her greatest regrets was that Jimmie never got to meet Lance. As for the scrawled message she left the head Mooseketeer at his hospital bed (the contents of which she never revealed), "I don't know if he saw it or not," she said in an interview later. "Ruth was very sweet. She told me he woke up during the night and saw the note. I hope he did."

There could have been no surer way to mark the official ending of the *Mickey Mouse Club* era than the death of the Mouseketeers' folksy, Christian hero, Jimmie Dodd. As Don says, "We represented wholesomeness. Those were the times. We represented the fifties, the wholesomeness we thought most kids were aspiring to." But now, almost a decade after *The Mickey Mouse Club* began, "we had that initial shock of going through the sixties when [our peers] didn't want to know us because we represented a moral code, too," Doreen recalls. "And so because of that, we were passé by the time sixty-two, sixty-three started out."

The Mouseketeers had given up their childhoods for stardom, and now they were the ultimate symbols of uncool. As they faced the rest of their lives without Mouse ears, some embraced their Disney pasts, while others fled. Their paths would lead them everywhere from infamous nude layouts in men's magazines to Broadway stints to criminal convictions. But every step of the way, the world never let them forget that they were once the merry Mouseketeers.

Chapter Eleven

Life After Mousehood

The former Mouseketeers rode in a parade float down Disneyland's Main Street for a homecoming of sorts: They were traveling the same route they'd once marched twenty-five years earlier for their public debut at the park's 1955 opening. Now well into their thirties, the former child stars were reveling in being back in the Disney spotlight in October 1980—the show now an iconic success, their place in TV history now indisputable. Screaming crowds, filled with fans wearing those trademark ears, called out to their onetime idols with joy.

"We had, like, groupies," Karen says. "That's when I realized how deeply this show hit the public, how important it was to so many people. It was like we were rock stars or something." The thirty-one ex-Mice, most of them decades away from their last time in the spotlight, had gathered for the occasion to soak up the adulation. They finally felt vindicated for all those years of childhood sweat, all that ear-wearing, all that post-stardom teasing...

Until their float ground to a sudden stop, breaking down, shattering the glow of their shining moment.

Then, as if that weren't enough of a blow to their swelling egos of a few moments earlier, an onlooker's voice rose from the temporarily silenced crowd: "The original Mouseketeers? I thought you guys were all dead!"

Luckily their hit reunion TV special proved otherwise. "It's not that the Mouseketeers have become seedy and decrepit," *Variety* said of the November 23, 1980, airing. "On the contrary, they're still an unusually peppy and healthy-looking bunch for the most part, a tribute to Disney's taste and judgment." Echoed *The Orange County Register*: "Their faces are lined, some hairlines are receding, and some have gray in their hair. But what do you expect? They haven't been teenagers for quite a while." The *Los Angeles Times* asked, "Could this troupe of middle-aged ex–child television heroes compete with cherished memories of the Mouseketeers?" and answered, "Walt Disney would have been proud."

The Mouseketeers were very much alive in fans' hearts, even if they had slipped from the constant public view under which they'd lived their school years. They had dispersed all over the globe since *The Mickey Mouse Club*, attaining solo fame and marrying into it, entertaining in Vietnam and fighting there, capitalizing on their Mouseketeer status and hiding from it, all the while remaining Mouseketeers, whether they liked it or not. Life after Mousehood brought its greatest challenges yet—devastating illnesses, tragic losses, and even jail time—but few would escape the shadow of the ears.

$$\smile$$

Doreen Tracey had been on the run from her *Mickey Mouse Club* image since she tore through Australia on that final Mouseketeer tour in 1959. And as she changed into her skin-tight T-shirt and skirt in a nurse's barracks in Saigon and prepared to take the stage, she felt sure she'd finally done it. She and her Filipino backing band, the Invaders, had choppered in to play for the U.S. Army's Seventh Cavalry in the middle of the Vietnam War's Tet Offensive in 1968.

Indeed, she thrilled the hungry-for-distraction crowd with a rendition of "Hold On, I'm Coming," her white go-go boots and mini a far cry from her *Mickey Mouse Club* uniform. But after her final number, "We Gotta Get Out of This Place," as she and the band were taking their bows, the inevitable happened: A pair of Mouseketeer ears appeared, being passed up and down the aisles. A guy smack in the middle of the crowd put them on—and started singing "The Mickey Mouse Club March," soon joined by the entire crowd, transported back to their childhoods thirteen years earlier.

At first, Doreen was crushed. Would she ever be known as anything except a Mouseketeer? And yet she felt a proud swelling in her throat and tears dampening her face in spite of herself. Nostalgia overtook her as the war-torn soldiers belted, "*M-I-C—See you real* soon!—K-E-Y—*Why? Because we like you!*" Who could deny the emotional impact of an audience full of warriors, mid-quagmire, with the world's most innocent song, from the world's most innocent kids' show, bubbling up from their memories and wafting out of their mouths? "Every time I performed, I wanted to get away from the Mouseketeer thing," Doreen says. "I wanted to identify as an entertainer on my own. But I couldn't escape my past."

Doreen was one of a handful of former Mice who would spend decades trying to elude *The Mickey Mouse Club*'s impact on their lives. Whether it was performing overseas, sexing up their wholesome image, falling into serious depression, or turning to a life of crime, however, every act—no matter how dark—landed them right back within the confines of the Magic Kingdom. In fact, the more they tried to escape their Disney past, the clingier the Mouse image got.

When Doreen returned to the States, she took a job doing promotional work for rocker Frank Zappa, but she'd soon become famous again—or at least infamous—thanks, alas, to *The Mickey Mouse Club*. After Jerry Bowles's 1976 where-are-they-now book *Forever Hold Your Banner High!* came out, she agreed to help men's magazine *Gallery* capitalize on renewed public interest in Mouseketeerdom—by posing nude. Encouraged by her deputy sheriff boyfriend at the time, she embraced the notoriety-making move, thinking it would distance her from the innocence of the Mouse image if not Mouseketeerdom itself. "I thought, 'Yeah, why not?'" she says. "I thought it would be pretty hot."

So there she appeared, in the December 1976 Special Holiday Issue, under the headline REMEMBER LITTLE DOREEN? with a huge, adorable picture of her from her later Mouseketeer days, her bangs shining and eyelashes batting beneath her Mouse ears. "From its premiere on October 3, 1955, to the end of its first run in 1957, the *Mouse Club* was the most popular kiddie show in the history of television," the introduction said. "One of the reasons for the show's incredible popularity was sexy Doreen Tracey, a saucer-faced charmer, who always seemed on the verge of bursting out of her Mouse-sweater."

The layout played the Mousketheme to its full effect, depicting the grown Doreen in pigtails, braless and pantiless in a white T-shirt with her name across the chest, in her Mouse hat and Mickey Mouse socks. "You get caught up in your own ego, not paying attention, not seeing the full repercussions," she says of the photo shoot. "You don't really look objectively, you get yourself in a lot of hot water. And so I lost a lot of shows at Disney. They used to call me two, three times a year for appearances before I did *Gallery*, and now they wouldn't touch me."

Resigned to her banned-from-Disney status, she posed again for the magazine in 1979, this time defiantly: Teased on the cover of the August issue as "Mouseketeer Doreen Back (and Front) by Popular Demand," this time the layout taunted Disney even more. She was shown in a barely existent white tank top—with her name across it Mouseketeer-style, of course—and, worse, flashing the camera while posing near the actual Walt Disney Productions employee entrance at 500 S. Buena Vista Street. "I went back and did it again just to show them I could do it," she says. "I'm in a trench coat. I'm walking at Alameda and Buena Vista—that used to be our parking lot where we would also play baseball. It was like six o'clock in the morning and the guard wasn't on duty when we shot it. And there's a big sign that says PROPERTY OF WALT DISNEY STUDIOS. I thought it was brilliant." The Walt Disney Company, on the other hand, didn't: "I was blackballed. They had my nude picture on all the executives' bulletin boards and they'd throw darts at it."

After Doreen made nice with Disney for the twenty-fifth anniversary in 1980, however, she became a Mouseketeer-event regular during the '90s. She retired from a longtime job as an administrator in the legal department at Warner Bros. Records in 2009 and is mulling over a new nightclub act. "And I've been trying to get a memoir done for years," she says. "But then a new chapter arises and I go, 'Oh, no, it's too early.'"

Lonnie Burr headed into similarly conflicted territory as he transitioned out of Mouseketeerdom and into real life. At first, he'd seemed on the exact right track: While making appearances on shows such as *The Beverly Hillbillies* and *Father Knows Best* in the late '60s, he sped through a bachelor's degree at California State University, Northridge, then headed to UCLA to get his master's in theater. He grew disillusioned by losing out on roles there to upperclassman David Birney (who'd go on to star in TV's *St. Else-where*), but he soldiered through and emerged with an MA by age twenty.

Soon thereafter, though, while Lonnie was living in the attic of his grandparents' house in Van Nuys, California, he fell into a deep depression. Despondent over a lack of direction in general as well as his girlfriend's recent rejection of his marriage proposal, he drank too much scotch one day and took out a bowie knife—he'd always carried pocketknives since he was twelve—and tried to cut his wrists. But he only ended up feeling woozy before a friend showed up and took Lonnie to the hospital to get stitched up with little lasting damage.

He credits the incident for turning his life around and forcing him into therapy, but he also attributes his depression to what he calls "showbizaphobia"—the emotional fallout of being a child actor. He says it wasn't easy continuing to pursue what he loved—acting, dancing, and singing—after feeling washed up at twenty. "I came back into the business," he says, "but I was typed as this little blond boy who dances very well, and I just couldn't get a shot."

Because of that, Lonnie spent years resenting his Mouseketeer past, grumbling in a 1976 interview, for instance, "I've done a lot of things since that are better and more creative. But the press always seems to fasten on that. If I said I was just Hamlet at Stratford and was sensational they'd say, 'Oh, yeah. Great. Now, tell me: What was Annette Funicello really like?'"

Still, he couldn't bring himself to give up acting. He's spent the decades post–*Mouse Club* plugging away in character parts on TV (*Chicago Hope, Lois and Clark*), in film (*Hook, Lionheart*), and on stage (*The Grapes of Wrath, 42nd Street*). Yet *The Mickey Mouse Club* would remain his longest single acting gig. It's taken a while, but he's come around to accepting his lifelong Mouse ears: He calls the series "emblematic of the good parts of the '50s." In addition to his memoir, *Confessions of an Accidental Mouseketeer,* he maintains by far the most extensive, and most Mousekecentric, website of all the Club alums: MouseketeerLonnieBurr.com.

Darlene Gillespie had even more reason to try to get away from *The Mickey Mouse Club* in general—and Annette in particular. As her closest Mouseketeer competitor had risen to icon status throughout the '60s, Darlene struggled to transcend her Disney experience. The pressure to do so bore down on her all the more because so many former costars and expectant fans assumed she, of all people, would find her rightful place in the entertainment world post–*Mickey Mouse Club,* with her stunning vocal talent and her sharp wit.

But once freed from her Disney recording contract, she released a single on Decca's Coral label called "I Loved, I Laughed, I Cried" in an effort to grow up and away from her Mouseketeer image. The record earned good reviews from *Billboard* but didn't make her a pop sensation. She worked on a nightclub act with her sisters, and ended up joining the Addrisi Brothers on a tour of Southern

California and Las Vegas in 1961, but never broke through as a solo act. She blipped back into pop-culture consciousness for a short time when she played Alice in Wonderland in a series of 1962 Ford commercials, then faded away once more.

She tried the normal, showbiz-free life for a time afterward, working as a surgical nurse at Valley Presbyterian Hospital. She later reported that, on occasion, a patient would say through the haze of anesthesia, "I know your voice. You're Darlene Gillespie, the Mouseketeer!" or that some colleagues would call her "Nurse Mouse"—neither of which went over well with her.

In 1968, she married gasoline-business tycoon Philip Gammon, who used his wealth to start a record company in hopes of launching a comeback for his new wife. Under the name Darlene Valentine, she cut several country songs in the '70s. Still, her career didn't quite achieve liftoff, and the couple, after having two kids, divorced in 1983. Darlene remained disenchanted with having been unable to rise above her Mouseketeer past. "Who wants to admit they were a fifteen-year-old Mouse?" she said to *TV Guide* in 1975. "If having been a Mouseketeer is the only thing I have to be remembered for," she lamented in 1979, "I'd just as soon be forgotten."

In fact, she began hinting at her retrospective disaffection with Disney's way of doing business in interviews throughout the '70s. "I didn't get anything extra for being featured in *Corky*, and I suspect—but can't prove it—that I've never gotten a fair count on overseas royalties from the records I did for them," she said in 1979.

"Christ, that *Alice in Wonderland* record has sold over a million copies. I see it every once in a while down at Ralphs supermarket. My father checked into it once and somebody at the studio told him, 'You're going to need a multimillionaire lawyer if you're going to take on Walt Disney.'"

Multimillionaire lawyer or no, she did just that in 1990, filing a lawsuit accusing the company of cheating her out of royalties. She claimed Disney promised a "substantial amount of money" from her share of merchandise sales and residuals and "failed to inform her that her actual realized earnings would be divided in such a way" that she would not receive "any more than a few dollars from the sales," which the suit estimated at more than $10 million. She maintained Disney had taken advantage of her young age and fraudulently promised she would become "a well-known artist," even though she never gained the same fame as Annette did. The Screen Actors Guild even backed her case, though she and Disney ended up settling out of court with undisclosed terms.

The same year Darlene filed the suit, however, she also met a guy named Jerry Fraschilla, with whom she ventured down a more unfortunate path. First Darlene and her beau were accused of taking up a fraudulent stock-buying practice, purchasing and then reselling stock without planning to pay for it, according to a 1994 suit filed against them by the Securities and Exchange Commission. The duo notched their first criminal conviction together in 1997 after showing up on store security cameras stealing a food processor and four shirts from a Macy's in Ventura, California. Allegations of fraud, lying under oath, and more fraud followed. By March 1999, Darlene—now married to Fraschilla—received a two-year sentence to federal prison for the SEC-related charges that she'd written fake checks and lied under oath. The headlines squealed with glee, never letting her forget her ties to *The Mickey Mouse Club* nearly half a century earlier: MOUSEKETEER FIANCÉ WON'T GET CHEESE. 1950S MOUSEKETEER'S ACT CALLED THEFT. TWO YEARS IN THE HOLE. B-U-S-T-E-D: MOUSEKETEER A SCAMMER.

David Stollery became one of a few former *Mickey Mouse Club* stars who averted self-destruction by doing the unthinkable: leaving stardom behind and focusing on fading into a life of sheer normalcy.

David had been lucky enough to always know just where his passion lay in life, and to know it was in designing cars, not performing. Still, he had an uncanny talent for acting that kept getting him more jobs even after he'd decided to study car design instead. "I had had a successful career," he says of his time in Hollywood. "Nothing unpleasant had happened to me. But pretty much early on, since the time I was five or six, I knew what I really wanted to do in life."

But once he was immersed in his schoolwork for his new career—his *real* career—he got a call from his former agent one day in 1961. "When you're on your way back from class, will you stop by this studio?" the agent said. "They're doing a series and I think you'd be just right."

"Listen," David, now twenty, said. "I'm not doing that."

"Just stop by. It won't hurt you."

Ever the amenable guy, David went, and ever the pro, he landed the part. Producers offered him a thirty-nine-week job at a thousand dollars a week, no small cash for a twenty-year-old in 1961. "Look, let's just shoot the pilot," the producer told him. "And if it doesn't go to series, you can still get the $39,000."

An undeniable deal. Still, David turned it down.

"I said, 'I cannot keep going back and forth,'" he recalls now. "At some time in your life you've got to say, 'I'm going to do this' or 'I'm going to do that.' Otherwise, all of a sudden you're thirty, you're forty, and you're fifty, and you're really not very good at this *or* that."

However, he does credit his acting career for instilling in him the quality that has benefited him most in his chosen field. "You know, there was no screwing around at Art Center College," he says. "There were no fraternities or sororities, and the people who went there wanted one thing, to be able to get through school with the highest grade average. And that was great." That competitive atmosphere, in turn, prepared him for his first job at General Motors in Detroit in 1964: "General Motors, at that time, had a fifty-six-percent market share. They paid less than other people who offered you jobs, but if you were one of the lucky few that got a job with GM, you took it. And it was the same thing. You're here on time and there's no screwing around outside of work. You're outside of work and you get picked up for disorderly conduct or being drunk, and you're out. By the time I left GM, I was thirty-one and I had just been in this deal where you might as well have been in prison." He is the rare breed of former child star who concludes of this arrangement: "I was so lucky. So lucky."

David was also under even more pressure than his coworkers, thanks to his *Mickey Mouse Club* heartthrob status. "When I was hired by General Motors Corporation, they hired me based on what I achieved in school," he says. "But there was still a little bit of trepidation over the fact that I had been this teenage actor. 'Is this guy just interested in the glamour of design and not a serious designer?' So I went in with a little bit of suspicion about me. 'Is he gonna show up? Is he gonna be hungover? Is he gonna come in and do the job?'" They had *no idea* what discipline it took to work for Disney.

He tried once to combine his love of design with his experience in show business by building the sets for the Steven Spielberg–produced, sci-fi television series *SeaQuest DSV* in 1993. "That was the first time I did anything like that for the entertainment industry," he says. "It was ridiculously challenging. I told them, 'Okay, we're going to get it done in this amount of time, here's how much it's going to cost,' and after about a week I'm looking at this thing going, 'I'm an idiot. There's no way I'm going to get this done. This time I've gone too far.' But I had to get it done because I would have been too embarrassed to call Steven Spielberg: 'Hey, Steve, I know you're in Poland shooting *Schindler's List,* but your series isn't happening, buddy.'" David got the job done, but it was the last time he'd work in Hollywood, save for a cameo with Tim Considine in a TV movie update of *Spin and Marty.*

Karen Pendleton didn't rush away from the spotlight with the same determination as David, but she did fall back into the comfort of obscurity without her kindred spirit, Cubby O'Brien, by her side. After the duo turned down Disney's joint contract in 1958 and Cubby went off to his instant professional drumming career, Karen toughed it out through the rest of her school years—though because of the continued Mouse-baiting her classmates indulged in, she never found her place. She tried college at Cal State Northridge for a while, but soon dropped out, determining school was just not her thing.

Acting, however, wasn't her thing either, which made a performing career difficult as well. Auditions made her too nervous, anyway. Her mother took her to try out for a role in the *West Side Story* film adaptation, but she wouldn't even go inside. "I did audition for a show in Vegas for short girls," the four-foot-ten dancer says. "They picked me, but they had to unpick me, because no one was as short as I was."

By 1970, Karen accepted that she wasn't cut out for show business. She settled into anonymity when she married Marine Mike DeLauer upon his return from Vietnam, and the two had a daughter.

She took a job at a May Department Store as a sales clerk, where she ran right into her Mouseketeer past: Both Annette's mother and a diamond-strewn Cheryl Holdridge, by then Mrs. Lance Reventlow, came into the store. They were friendly, but Karen grew embarrassed about how ordinary her life had turned out. "I felt like, 'Oh, sure, things are going great with me!'" she quips.

After moving to Fresno in Central California and splitting with her husband, Karen suffered a far more devastating blow: a car crash that injured her spinal cord and left her paraplegic, putting the former dancer in a wheelchair. The accident, however, also marked the beginning of a courageous new chapter in her life. The shy and anxious former Mouse finished both her bachelor's and master's degrees in psychology while also a single mom, spurred to provide a better life for herself and her daughter. She worked at a battered women's shelter, then at the Center for Independent Living in Fresno, where she still lives. Through it all, she leaned on her former costars for help: David, Doreen, Cheryl, and Tommy appeared at fund-raisers for the center, and Darlene came to her aid early and often during her recovery, taking her to specialists and providing moral support. "I had no money, I was split with my husband," Karen recalls. "They did a lot for me."

Mary Espinosa retreated from Hollywood too, though she didn't go happily. It took her decades to make peace with the monumental rejection of getting kicked off the show at such a formative age:

"I think we all went through a period of denial," she says, "some shorter and some longer." After she left *The Mickey Mouse Club* in 1956, she didn't return to show business, keeping her performing urges to community theater and high school musicals. She got married at twenty and had two kids in quick succession before divorcing in her late twenties, when she got a job in personnel administration.

She participated in the twenty-fifth anniversary celebration like all of the other former Mouseketeers and took pride in saying her name in Roll Call the way she never got to on the show, since she was part of the second-string Blue Team. "It was really exciting," she says. "And it was really cute to see it. But I saw it and I thought, 'That's why they let me go,' because I wouldn't look right into the camera. My eyes were, like, blinking."

However, she found that because of her ouster from the show more than two decades earlier, she didn't like being at Disneyland for that event—or for any other reason. "I didn't even want to go to Disneyland," she says. "I didn't want to be in that realm, because I felt like I was a failure because I got dropped." However, after appearing there for the 1980 event, she decided that instead of avoiding the Happiest Place on Earth for the rest of her life, she should deal with the long-buried anxiety her return to the amusement park unearthed. To do that, she joined the controversial self-help seminar program Landmark Education. "Through Landmark I got complete with that conversation that I had been a failure— they look at everything in life as a conversation," she says. "And then I created the possibility of getting back in touch with Disney, so I called Lonnie. He said Disney was planning a fiftieth celebration and put me in touch with the people planning it. After that call they invited me back, and I did the fiftieth birthday party celebration onstage at Disneyland, for a week. It was amazing."

As part of what she calls her "healing process," she's also worked as an extra on several television shows, including *L.A. Law*. "Any soundstage still smells the same," she says. "Going on a set is always like coming home."

Tommy Cole, like many former Mice who took up behind-the-scenes careers, never wanted to give up on-set life either—despite deciding to leave performing behind for good. Just after returning from a six-month stint in the Air Force in 1963, the twenty-one-year-old started losing hope in a solo singing career as British rockers supplanted balladeers like him on the charts. In 1965, he embarked on what would be his final gig, as a backup singer for a Johnny Mathis tour through Korea. It would prove a fortuitous job even if it didn't lead to a career as a crooner: He met his wife, Aileen, a New York–based dancer at the time, on a tour stop in Seoul. "I saw this cute little thing doing backflips in the street, and that was my wife-to-be," he says. "So I followed her and I made a date with her for the next day, and we went out. But I didn't see her again for a year. I kept her number, but I had a girlfriend from back here. I broke up with the gal about a year later. And I wrote Aileen a letter. It took about two years, then we got married."

Settling down inspired him to choose a stable career as a makeup artist, inspired by his time on the *My Three Sons* set. Apprenticeships at ABC and NBC led to the first movie on which he headed up the makeup department—1977's Disney film *Pete's Dragon*, which was shot on none other than Sound Stage 1, the Mouseketeers' onetime home base. "I'd get these memories when I'd come on the stage," he says. "There were stairs going up, and I could suddenly remember Darlene going up to the sound booth, going in and turning on the light, and being loud on the mic." He won an Emmy for makeup design on the 1979 miniseries *Backstairs at the White House*, and was nominated six other times. He'd be the only Mouseketeer to ever win a major entertainment-industry award.

Tommy remains involved in the inner workings of Hollywood, representing the Makeup Artists and Hairstylists Guild on the board of the television academy, relishing still being at the center of the industry in which he grew up. People often recognize his name as that of a former Mouseketeer at industry conventions and gatherings, and he doesn't mind a bit. "They look at me and say, 'Thank you for being our babysitter,' or 'Thank you for all the entertainment.' I'm sixty-seven years old, and to be recognized for something I did over fifty years ago, and with a smile, is kind of neat."

*   *   *

Sharon Baird found an altogether different way of capitalizing on both her Mouseketeer résumé and her natural gifts to remain in Hollywood post–*Mickey Mouse Club*—even without achieving superstardom. When she emerged from her school years, she found that her bread and butter—variety shows—weren't doing the business they used to. But after working an office job for a few years, she stumbled upon a way to stay in show business after all: Her tiny stature got her work on children's shows as costumed characters. Starting in 1969, a whole new part of Hollywood opened up to her. She appeared on *The New Zoo Revue, H.R. Pufnstuf,* and *Land of the Lost,* among other shows, as well as *Welcome to Pooh Corner* and *Dumbo Circus* for the Disney Channel. She even played the title character in 1986's critically derided, cult-beloved film *Ratboy,* credited as S. L. Baird so no one knew that under all the heavy makeup and costuming was a Mousegirl instead. "I was able to be on shows and in movies that were popular," she says of her costumed career, "and still go to the market and just do whatever I wanted to do without being recognized by fans. I was still dancing and doing my thing without worrying about any of that."

These days, she's retired to Reno, Nevada, where she has a whole room of her house dedicated to *Mickey Mouse Club* memorabilia. She still maintains a part-time job in a nail salon, a line of work she chose so she could continue being a Mouseketeer whenever she wants to. "Your hours are your own," she says. "So when we do reunion shows or conventions or something like that, I can go without a problem. It works out well."

A few former Mice, however, wanted to find bigger fame—and were lucky enough to do so, at least for a while. Cheryl Holdridge was chief among them: In the years leading up to her 1964 marriage to millionaire Lance Reventlow, her California-girl looks and sweet demeanor garnered her an enviable career, most notably as Wally's girlfriend, Julie, on *Leave It to Beaver*. "Cheryl was very bright," Doreen now remembers. "She knew that she was never the best dancer or singer. But she knew she *was* the American Dream. Gorgeous."

Cheryl became a famously wealthy wife when she married Reventlow, and then a famously wealthy widow when he died in a skiing accident in 1972. She married twice more, but for the most part disappeared from the Hollywood scene—aside from appearances with her former *Mickey Mouse Club* costars—until her death from lung cancer in 2009. "She loved being a wife and she took care of her men," Doreen says. "And this is the one who could have been like an Angelina Jolie if she'd continued with her career." Adds Tommy Cole, "She was a bright star in our family, in the sense that she'd walk into a doorway and just light up the door, light up the room."

*   *   *

Sherry Alberoni (Allen to *Mouse Club* fans) became another sit-com bombshell. She did the rounds of guest spots on *My Three Sons*, *The Monkees*, and *The Donna Reed Show* before landing a longer-running part as Cissy's friend Sharon James on *Family Affair*. She also appeared on *The Dating Game*, and like her stint on *My Three Sons*, she appeared multiple times: "One time I had red hair, one time I was a blonde, and one time I was a brunette." Then, when her TV career started to wane, she finally put her trademark lisp to good use when she started lending her distinctive voice to cartoons such as *Josie and the Pussycats*, *Super Friends*, and *The Mighty Orbots*.

Despite her greater fame on other shows, she remained a loyal ex-Mouseketeer—taking a bigger role as a former cast member than she ever did during her brief season on the show—and even married a devoted *Mouse Club* fan, a doctor named Richard Van Meter. "My husband was a little army brat in Germany and he was watching it," she says. "He remembers watching me—Karen, Cubby, and myself, the youngest, the little tiny kids. Kids remember watching it, literally around the world."

Tim Considine, on the other hand, could never quite accept his place in the sitcom-kid factory. After the erstwhile Spin played oldest-brother Mike Douglas on *My Three Sons* for five years, he declared himself "retired" from acting yet again, just as he'd done before *and* after starring in *The Adventures of Spin and Marty*. In 1965, he decided he wanted to leave the business because—having written two episodes and directed a few scenes—he wanted to get behind the camera more. When producer Don Fedderson declined to let him do so, the twenty-four-year-old Tim walked. "They didn't need me," he says. "It went on for seven years without me. I just tired of it. I'd had it. And I said, 'Well, I'm out.' It wasn't that I hated anybody or anything. I just wasn't that interested in doing the same thing over again."

The incident marked the only time Tim's mother ever questioned his decision to quit a role. "It was a job, it was an occupation by then," he explains. "She said, 'Are you sure you want to do that? You've got an awfully good thing going.' That was the first word ever."

He, of course, didn't listen. He'd retreat into writing—first for TV with his brother, John. "But again there was something about that I didn't care for," Tim says. "I wasn't very good at the meetings and stuff like that. My brother and I would go into a meeting and [producers] would say, 'Oh, we love the script, great job, *but* can we make the leading lady a monkey?' At which point I would go, 'What?' And my brother would say, 'That's okay, it's okay, Tim.' It just became too much of a strain so I stopped doing that. I don't like other people saying, 'Change this, change that.'"

Tim ended up, at last, finding a profession he felt he could control enough to make him happy: freelance writing—in particular about his longtime passion, fast cars, which has allowed him to author several articles about his costar-turned-automotive-designer David Stollery. "I don't work for anybody," Tim says. "I pitch the stories, and [publications] either buy them or they don't. I like that."

Tim's TV little brother, Don Grady, stuck with *My Three Sons* well past Tim's departure in 1965, morphing from the discouraged middle sibling to the self-assured oldest. For him, the series was a far more important stepping stone than the *Mouse Club*, allowing him to showcase his acting as well as his musical talents when his own band, the Greefs, made an appearance on the show with him. "I've always loved music," Don says. "I've always had a passion. And so when the *Three Sons* stuff was over, I couldn't wait to get into something I was passionate about. I never really saw myself as an actor. It was just something that happened out of my musical beginning."

Once he left *My Three Sons*, Don launched a full-time music career, writing scores for movies, television, and stage. He also met his wife, Ginny, whom he married in 1985, thanks to his Mouseketeerdom. The two both participated in a Disneyland stage show that pitted original Mouseketeers against "new" ones—younger hired performers—in a dance-off. "It was Bobby, Sharon, and me, and then three other young Mouseketeers," he says. "And she represented one of the new Mouseketeers. Of course the old Mouseketeers won, and, you know, I won because I met my wife."

Don continued to make music, and has even gone back to work for Disney several times, scoring all of its recent Disney Princess albums, as well as bonus music on special-release DVDs of *The Lion King* and *Aladdin*. In 2008, he released a jazz album, his first since 1973's *Homegrown*, aimed straight at the generation that grew up watching him on television—called, of course, *Boomer*. "Music today isn't speaking to us, the Baby Boomers, anymore," he says. "They're speaking to the younger generation because that's where the money is. But there's a huge generation of people like me who love music and want to hear about the things that we're going through."

Cubby O'Brien, too, settled into a comfortable lifelong show-business groove thanks to his musical abilities. In fact, he became the rare drummer to make a living in music—without the rock 'n' roll excess. After playing for *Lawrence Welk* for a few years, he graduated from Hollywood Professional School and then went on to provide beats for satirical bandleader Spike Jones, playing Vegas lounges at a mere sixteen years old, his mom coming out to Sin City to chaperone. By nineteen he'd gotten in on Ann-Margret's

Tahoe act, and had gotten married. "Not to Ann-Margret, though I tried very hard," he jokes. "There was this silver jumpsuit that was really getting to me."

He had, in fact, met first wife Marilyn Miller, a twenty-three-year-old vocalist with the Good Time Singers, while they were on Jones's tour together. They married in 1966 and had a daughter, Alicia, in 1969, while Cubby was serving as musical director for a Los Angeles production of *Hair* and drumming for *The Carol Burnett Show*. He hit the road with the Carpenters soon thereafter, embarking on a traveling-man lifestyle that hampered his relationship with Alicia until she reached adulthood: "I had some issues with my daughter because I wasn't there. I missed a lot of her activities, her proms and her things that girls want their dads to go to. If I'm with the Carpenters and they're doing a tour of Japan, I can't say to Karen and Richard, 'Hey, I can't do the Japan tour in five weeks because my daughter's going to be graduating.' I mean, you've got to pay the bills, you've got to go on the road, you've got to keep your career going. It's not easy."

In fact, his marriage to Alicia's mother disintegrated after just six years because of such strain. After the split, he traversed the country drumming for the likes of Bernadette Peters, Andy Williams, Joel Grey, and Shirley MacLaine. A touring production of *West Side Story* ended his twenty-one-year marriage to second wife Terri, who wanted to stay put and make a life in Texas, but the divorce freed Cubby to move to New York to pursue a new avenue in his career: Broadway. He'd go on to play for the long-running

phenomenon *The Producers* as well as Peters's revival of *Gypsy*.
During that time he also met the woman he calls his "true soul
mate," current wife, Holly.

Now semi-retired in Oregon thanks to his Musicians Union
pension, Cubby continues to tour from time to time with Peters,
who never fails to honor his Mouseketeer past. "Bernadette even
now introduces me as, 'We have a celebrity in this orchestra. He's
a great tap dancer, he's a great husband, he's a great drummer, and
he's one of the famous Mouseketeers.' We were all out to dinner the
other night and she said, 'You know, you were my favorite Mouseketeer when I was watching as a kid. You were so cute.' I've known
her now for forty years, but I never knew that."

Cubby's fellow *Lawrence Welk* star, Bobby Burgess, had even less
of a compunction to escape his Mouse past. He's spent his entire
life beaming through the same kinds of dance routines that got
him noticed on *The Mickey Mouse Club*, having found another
comfortable, longtime television home on *Welk* starting in 1961.
Bobby stuck with *Welk* until it ended in 1982 and returned for its
yearly specials ever after.

He's still dancing to this day, teaching ballroom steps to soci-
ety boys and girls at Burgess Cotillion in his hometown of Long
Beach, with *The Mickey Mouse Club* still getting top billing on his
decades-long résumé, and his wife, Kristin, whom he met on *Welk*,
still getting props as "his favorite dancing partner." A creature of

habit, Bobby likes the long-term gigs his dancing has afforded him: "I appreciate it," he says. "I don't like auditions."

Even Queen Mouse Annette Funicello could never quite move beyond her *Mickey Mouse Club* image—even though she'd also become an icon in her own right. She cemented her place in pop culture history when she signed on to star in 1963's *Beach Party*, her first major foray into non-Disneyfied territory. The bikini flick sexed up her image while still depicting sunny, clean California fun—just what you'd expect a former Mouseketeer to do with her early twenties, but just enough to take her beyond Disney's world.

Longtime mentor Walt gave her a stern talk before she left the Magic Kingdom for the Southern California surf, asking her to make sure she maintained her innocent image and issuing his infamous plea to keep her navel covered. The historic record shows that she did her best to comply (despite a few navel slipups), and *Beach Party*'s success led to a string of sand-and-surf films featuring Annette and on-screen boyfriend Frankie Avalon. The two became so associated with each other in the cultural ether that fans would continue to think, for decades to come, that they were a real couple.

But in fact, in 1965, Annette, then twenty-two, married her International Creative Management agent, Jack Gilardi, whom she'd met on the set of *Babes in Toyland*. She had three children with him during their sixteen-year marriage. (Mickey Mouse—that is, a Disney-hired employee in costume—attended both of her weddings, as well as the birth of her first child.) After her final beach movie, 1967's *Thunder Alley,* Annette downshifted to motherhood full-time. "That young girl in the little black Mouse ears, that highly principled, buxom young lady singing and pouting over Frankie out on the beach—*that* was Annette," she writes. "To my family and my closest friends, I was just Annie."

She would, however, be thrust back into the spotlight for the most unfortunate of reasons: her 1987 diagnosis of multiple sclerosis. Just before then, things had been going well for the star, who'd divorced her first husband but had recently remarried to racehorse breeder Glen Holt and released a country album. But she'd quietly been suffering ever-increasing symptoms—blurred vision, weakness, tingling, memory problems, fatigue. She tried to keep her illness a secret as she went through with plans for a reunion concert tour with Frankie Avalon in 1989 and 1990, weaving elaborate lies about bad knees and tendonitis to all but her family and closest friends. "I guess it was the fact that the public has always been on my side that led me to keep my struggle with multiple sclerosis a secret for over five years," she writes. "After all, nothing bad could ever happen to Annette." She wore a knee brace so she could present solid visual evidence of some likely excuse, and, for a while, kept her disease hidden from even her father for fear of worrying him.

Soon enough, though, those closest to her, including her former

Mickey Mouse Club costars, started to notice something was awry. "Annie and I were dancing together in 1990 down in Florida for a show with the new Mouseketeers," Tommy recalls. "We were dancing a fairly intricate number. We were all still pretty good dancers, but Annie kept missing steps, just little trips. I knew something was wrong, but I didn't know what was wrong. Glen was saying, 'Oh, she just had surgery a while back, so she's still recovering from that.' But I still knew there was something wrong." The stress of covering up her condition only made it worse, and soon she was having trouble with basic tasks like walking or getting up from a chair. One of her son's friends even said, after spotting her stumbling while out to dinner, "I saw your mom leaving the restaurant last night, and, boy, did she have one too many."

Tabloid reporters started coming to the same conclusion. When Annette got calls at home from reporters asking what was wrong with her, she took control of the story herself by telling it to a trusted writer at *USA Today*, a move she calls "one of the most agonizing decisions of my life....I worried that all those kind folks—from adults who'd been Mouseketeers First Class in Good Standing back in the '50s to the young kids who had attended my last concert tour with Frankie Avalon in 1989–90—would discover that Annette's life was not quite the happy Disney fairy tale they believed and feel somehow betrayed. I had known and felt their love almost all my life; I didn't want their pity now."

What she gained, however, was immense respect and support from her fans, the Disney family, and Hollywood at large. That same year, she was named a Disney Legend (alongside posthumous honors for Jimmie Dodd and Roy Williams). She got her Hollywood Walk of Fame star a year later, in 1993, when she was already relegated to a wheelchair and walker. Mickey Mouse, of course, was there. "Mickey Mouse is my best friend," she said in an interview on the occasion. "He's been there for every important occasion of my life. I'm lucky in this life because of Walt Disney." That same year, she still managed to promote a boxed set of her Walt Disney records and launch both a perfume and a teddy bear line. She also started the Annette Funicello Research Fund for Neurological Diseases. "You learn to live with it," she said on the talk show *John & Leeza*. "You learn to live with anything—you really do." In 1994, she released her memoir, and a year later helped shape a TV biopic of her life based on the book.

These days, she can't talk or walk much, but she's still fighting her debilitating disease with support from husband Glen, according to several of her fellow Mouseketeers who still keep in touch with her on a regular basis. "She's still the love of our lives," Tommy says. "She's still the beautiful brunette everybody knew."

By the time the Mouseketeers' fiftieth anniversary celebration came to pass, Annette could no longer join in the festivities. But Karen proudly appeared in *her* wheelchair, dancing alongside nine other former Mice at Disneyland. Cubby, Sherry, Karen, Doreen, Sharon,

Don, Bobby, Cheryl, Tommy, and Mary all performed in sparkly black Mouse ears and white mock turtleneck sweaters embroidered with their names. Afterward, they unveiled the "world's largest pair of Mouseketeer ears"—that is, a thousand fans standing in that recognizable shape in front of Sleeping Beauty Castle. Who knew, when they first saw those beanies so many years earlier, that they would last so long as an image? Or, as many of the Mice see it, would haunt them for eternity? "It bothers me that we still have to wear them," Karen says with a sigh. "But at least they make them fancy and put glitter on them now."

Many former Mice hadn't seen one another or talked in some time, but it all came right back: kidding Bobby about his cartoon smile or Tommy about his loss of hair (which, as Cubby says, "has always been a big part of his life"). They got to dance and sing as most of them hadn't gotten to do in years. "I got this chubby body up and did a little dancing, a little singing," Tommy says. "We really enjoy working together. There's a core of us who just still enjoy each other. We have fun." Adulthood also allowed Mouseketeers whose paths never crossed during their Club stints to meet for the first time, like the best high school reunion. "I didn't know Cheryl, but at the fiftieth party we got to know each other," Mary says. "She was so generous—she bought me a beautiful Mickey Mouse pin with diamonds on it from Disneyland. It was wonderful. I wish I'd known her more."

Thrilled to show the world they had survived so much of life with their Mouseketeer pride intact, the group performed a seventeen-minute show with a live band, complete with "The Mickey Mouse Club March," Roll Call, a Sharon-and-Bobby dance to "Sweet Shop Rock," and renditions of "We Are the Merry Mouseketeers" as well as the "Talent Round-Up" song—the first song they ever performed together at Disneyland. Many wondered if it would be their last true celebration of Mouseketeerdom together at the place where it had all begun.

Then again, continuing to show up had become the Mouseketeer way, as much a part of them as their trademark ears and sweaters. But reunions and public appearances aren't the only way they've stuck around. Their influence pervades every part of the entertainment world even now. Today's youth-driven pop-culture landscape owes a lot to that moment in 1955 when those tiny Mice marched down Disneyland's Main Street, confusing fans and TV announcers who couldn't make heads or tails of those strange, winged hats or that curious moniker: Mouseketeers.

Chapter Twelve

The Mouseketeer Legacy

New and old Mouseketeers were coming together for the first time. The 1990s Mouseketeer revival was in full swing, with a hyper-modernized version of the original *Mickey Mouse Club* enthralling kids across the nation once more. The fresh-faced sensations were set to honor their 1950s forebears with a nostalgic alumni day on the Disney Channel hit show, so a group of former Mice ventured back to a place they never thought they'd be again: the Mouseketeer stage. Except this time, it was in Orlando, Florida, with a studio audience full of screaming kids, a malt shop set painted in an explosion of colors, a neon Mickey Mouse blinking overhead, and teen stars in slick letterman-style jackets—no sweaters, no Mouse ears—singing and dancing all around them. "I remember the new Mice as being very hip," Don says. "The original Mice certainly weren't hip. And we didn't have to worry about clothes. We had the uniform. But uniforms weren't appropriate in the nineties, and, unfortunately, neither were ears. I missed the ears on the new kids."

It was thirty-five years after the original *Mickey Mouse Club*'s debut, and Disney had recently revitalized the show with an updated format known to new fans as MMC. Sherry, Don, Tommy, Bobby, Sharon, and Annette showed up on the newfangled set—smack in the heart of Disney World—to be honored by their modern-day heirs on the air.

Some of the old-guard Mice enjoyed the infusion of enthusiasm they got from the kids, even though they felt something was missing in the translation. "I loved their energy," Don says. "Unlike the 'pack' that we were, they were reveling in their individuality, in the spirit of a newer age. For me, I did not feel a group consciousness about them, for better or for worse." The kids' rambunctiousness bewildered others of the former Mice. "The crew called us 'the pros,'" Sherry recalls. "They'd say, 'Okay, bring the pros in.' Because we were raised that you knew where your stage mark was, and you stood there, and you knew when you come in. And when we did MMC, what a group of talented kids, but they didn't know what a mark was, they knew nothing about lighting."

Things reached a fever pitch when then-fifteen-year-old Damon Pampolina, having not eaten all day, gorged on M&Ms and Coke before hitting the stage with a sugar rush, then passed out on the set when his blood sugar dropped. The incident made an *Orlando Sentinel* piece the next day that criticized producers of MMC for not running a tighter ship, and the elder Mouseketeers couldn't have agreed more. "There was no sense of 'time is money,' no sense of you've got a crew of men and women who are working for their pay, feeding their families, so you don't waste their time," Sherry says. "That was sad, to see how it had evolved. You know, screwing around, reading the lines wrong, making jokes. I really resented it."

The original Mouseketeers had been watching the new *Mickey Mouse Club* closely as it became a hit for a new generation. The old guard loved that kids were finally talking about Mouseketeers again, buying up albums and crowding concert appearances featuring the new Club members. But when the '50s Mouseketeers tuned in to the Disney Channel to see what all the fuss was about, many found it overproduced for their tastes. "I always thought they were trying to do something that could never be done again," Cubby says. "It had nothing to do with the *Mickey Mouse Club* I was on; it was just some new show they were calling *The Mickey Mouse Club*. It wasn't the same thing."

Adds Lonnie Burr, "We were all regular kids, really. That's part of the ingeniousness of the original that didn't happen in the second and third versions. They were too Vegas. We were just playing ourselves. That's one of the reasons kids related to it—Walt said everyone could be a Mouseketeer, and we were pleasant and ordinary enough that it wasn't like you had to do everything 100 percent better than everybody else." Cubby missed the original's moral compass as well: "The little things that Jimmie Dodd used to sing about, like 'Do What the Good Book Says,' forget it! Would they ever be able to say that on TV now?"

MMC might not have preached the same ideals or even looked

much like the '50s version, but it proved one thing: The original *Mickey Mouse Club* had been on to something almost half a century earlier. While the original Mouseketeers found MMC jarring and too glossy, the new production showed how innovative *The Mickey Mouse Club* had been way back in 1955 in giving kids a variety show just for them, populated by kids just like them. The rest of the world simply took a few decades to catch up.

Almost immediately after its original cancellation, *The Mickey Mouse Club* proved it had a reservoir of untapped staying power ABC executives hadn't counted on when they booted it off the air. The show kept coming back to television, in different forms, repackaged and recut and syndicated and supplemented, but always for the same reason: Kids liked Mouseketeers. Despite being canceled for supposed lack of interest and advertising revenue, it ran in syndication just four years later, enchanting a new generation as well as kids across the globe in eighteen countries.

By the mid-1970s Disney decided to revive the Mousekefever by creating *The All New Mickey Mouse Club*. The 1977 version would boast a multiracial group of performers—in fact, the show would boast about it over and over in all of the pre-show publicity—though the biggest breakouts would end up being blond, Farrah Fawcett–era stunners Julie Piekarski and Lisa Whelchel, both of whom would go on to star in boarding-school dramedy *The Facts of Life*. The new version of the show made no secret of its ties to the original: The theme song was a disco version of the original march. The new director, Josh White, had a go-to joke: "Here they are, folks, the new and amazing Mouseketeers, performing feats of derring-do without a net!" Get it? *Annette!*

The new series, however, couldn't recapture the magic of the original. It ended just six months after it began, topping out at 130 half-hour shows, never picking up a wide enough syndication run to make it a phenomenon. Though it ran in limited reruns until January 1979, unlike its predecessor, it faded quickly from audiences' memories. "I knew one of the directors, and I came and watched one of the tapings," says former Mouse Eileen Rogosin (née Diamond), who was by then working in Hollywood as a casting agent. "I thought, 'This is really not good.' I don't think there was anything like the first one."

Still, Disney ventured back into the Mouse business one more time in the 1990s. The time finally felt right, with Disney now owning its own pay cable venture, the Disney Channel, which was struggling to find a defining hit and had twenty-four hours of wide-open airtime. Disney would also control the show all on its own, unlike when it had to answer to ABC in the '50s or syndicators in the '70s. And the kid market had come into its own as a driving force in the industry, as evidenced by the launch of youthful competing cable channel Nickelodeon and its hip, junior-sketch-comedy hit, *You Can't Do That on Television*. In an entertainment environment now driven by niche programming—cable companies offered an average of eighty channels at the time—and in a marketplace that had learned the marketing power of the youth audience, the newest revival, MMC, would finally realize the full potential of the franchise. It would last for seven seasons, finding success with a new generation by cribbing as much from more contemporary TV formats such as late-night staple *Saturday Night Live* as it did from the original *Mickey Mouse Club.*

This version, though, added music-video-style production numbers and cover versions of hit pop songs to target a somewhat older audience than the original. Theme days got updates—Circus Day became Party Day, Talent Round-Up turned into Hall of Fame Day (honoring regular kids for various achievements), Guest Star Day morphed into just Guest Day (granting wishes to MMC viewers who wrote in)—and the romantic serial *Teen Angel*, starring a pre–*Beverly Hills, 90210* Jason Priestley, replaced the more rough-and-tumble serials such as *Spin and Marty.*

The updated formula worked—young audiences were finally idolizing a new generation of Disney-bred stars. The new version would, in fact, go down in history as a star-finding machine. A little blond powerhouse singer named Christina Aguilera was the golden-voiced MMC equivalent of Darlene Gillespie; small-town Louisiana kid Britney Spears was the everygirl with middling vocal chops, killer dance skills, and loads of sex appeal, à la Annette Funicello. Charmer Justin Timberlake was Lonnie Burr, Tommy Cole, and Tim Considine in one—a heartthrob who could sing, dance, and steal a scene. The massive talents the whole world would discover a few years later had millions of kids across the country glued to their televisions once again, every weekday evening. Just as *The Mickey Mouse Club* had put Disney on the television map, MMC had made the Disney Channel a real cable player. Disney had recaptured the kid-TV kingdom thirty-five years later, and in doing so had rediscovered that its original model for teen star-building, *The Mickey Mouse Club*, could work with a few modern tweaks.

This time around, though, MMC alumni would take Hollywood by storm almost instantly upon graduating from Mouseketeerhood. Christina would go on to sell 25 million albums worldwide and win four Grammy Awards as of 2010, while Britney would become a tabloid-target phenomenon who'd score the best-selling album ever for a teenage solo artist with her 1999 debut, . . . *Baby One More Time*, and would dominate the decade to come. Justin went from boy band wonder with *N Sync to solo superstar. The cast at the time also included future Oscar nominee Ryan Gosling and *Felicity* star Keri Russell. Even among the show's rejected auditioners were the likes of box-office draw Matt Damon and pop singer Jessica Simpson.

It turned out Disney had been right nearly four decades earlier: Children were an economic force worth tapping, and there was no better way to tap into their passion than by making a TV show for kids, starring kids. Give young audiences stars of their own, and they will consume anything and everything to do with those kid idols. The original *Mickey Mouse Club* invented the possibility that a star could be a schoolyard name—famous only among the elementary and junior high set—before becoming a household name. It proved kids were worth programming for *and* worth watching.

In fact, the model pioneered by the Mouseketeers once upon a time might now even be growing too successful for its own good—or at least its stars' own good. With the Disney Channel churning out kiddie superstars like Miley Cyrus and *High School Musical*'s Zac Efron twenty-four hours a day—and former MMCers dominating the pop-culture landscape—the original '50s Mouseketeers can only watch in wonder, relieved, for the most part, that they never had to wrestle with such overwhelming stardom, as much as many of them had wished for just that at the time. "Now I see these young entertainers, and it's too much too fast," David Stollery says. "We were lucky at that time, that we didn't have this incredible adulation and money. We had more than the average kid, but it wasn't on this scale that you just couldn't deal with."

Cubby regards Mouseketeerdom as a symbol of all that was good about the '50s, and all that's gone wrong with kid stars in the modern, paparazzi-driven age: "It was a different time. It wasn't that slick. We were just regular kids who had some talent, and other regular kids were looking and going, 'Yeah, maybe I could do that, maybe I could be a Mouseketeer too.' Nowadays when you look at somebody like that [kids on television] you don't really say to yourself, 'I could do that.' It's more like, 'I wouldn't want to do that,' because it's just too much of a hassle."

Such feelings make another iteration of *The Mickey Mouse Club* all the more unlikely, as does the current Disney star system, which switched from hoping for a breakout star to spring from the original cast to breeding modern-day Annette Funicellos from the start with MMC. "They each seemed to be striking out on their own,"

Don says of the '90s Mouseketeers. "When we, the old Mice, get together, the group identity re-forms immediately. It's a great bond. I wonder if the new Mice experience that."

With the channel now driven by nothing but star vehicles such as Miley Cyrus's *Hannah Montana* and Selena Gomez's *The Wizards of Waverly Place*, it's hard to imagine what another *Mickey Mouse Club* revival might look like. Disney executives won't comment on whether they'd ever attempt one; and even if they did launch another version, times have changed so much that it would likely be virtually unrecognizable as being derived from the original. "They already showed [with MMC] that you can't put the ears on Mouseketeers anymore," Don says. "What would go next?"

Those kids marching down Disneyland's Main Street whom the opening day announcers couldn't quite make sense of were the first, and in many ways only, club that was *truly* "made for you and me." As Lonnie says of himself and his castmates: "The kids were real enough to seem like buddies and friends as opposed to somebody who's this special person. *Everybody* could be part of our club and sing along." And even if it's a club that will likely never be again, we can still all sing along with those original Mouseketeers—and enjoy a trip back to a world where Mouse ears and sweaters were standard, Jimmie Dodd could solve any problem, and Annette was the love of everyone's life.

Appendix

Mickey Mouse Club Stars

Don Agrati (aka Don Grady): The third-season replacement Mouseketeer, thirteen years old during his time on the show, got lots of screen time after joining the cast in 1957 even though he never made the first-string Red Team. Because he came to the show so late in its run, he found much greater fame in his post–*Mickey Mouse Club* life—after changing his last name from Agrati to Grady—thanks mostly to an eleven-year run as middle brother Robbie Douglas on *My Three Sons*. He became a musician afterward, playing with bands such as the Greefs and Yellow Balloon before finding steady work as a composer for television, films, and stage shows. He released a solo jazz album entitled *Boomer* in 2008.

Sherry Alberoni (aka Sherry Allen): Sherry, who had modeled and done a little acting when she was hired at just nine years old as a Mouseketeer, didn't gain much stardom during her brief second-season run (during which she was known by a stage name, Sherry Allen). But she went on to appear on a slew of 1960s sitcoms—

having changed back to her given last name, Alberoni—including *My Three Sons*, *The Man from U.N.C.L.E.*, *The Monkees*, and *A Family Affair* (her best-known role, as family friend Sharon James). She subsequently found career longevity doing voice work for animated series such as *Josie and the Pussycats*, *Super Friends*, and *The Mighty Orbots*.

Sharon Baird: The Mouseketeers' standout female dancer performed on the first-string Red Team for the show's entire three-year run. She came to *The Mickey Mouse Club* at eleven years old with an impressive amount of experience, including appearances in films such as *Bloodhounds of Broadway* and *Artists and Models*, as well as on television shows like *The Colgate Comedy Hour*. After a brief, post–*Mouse Club* stint in a nightclub act, she found a steady career in dressing as costumed characters for children's shows, including *The New Zoo Revue*, *H.R. Pufnstuf*, and *Land of the Lost*. She's now retired in Reno, Nevada.

Bobby Burgess: A former amateur contest champion thanks to his impeccable dance skills, Bobby had his first professional job at fourteen on *The Mickey Mouse Club*. While attending Long Beach State University after the show ended, he won yet another contest with dance partner Barbara Boylan that got the two a guest spot on *The Lawrence Welk Show*. Fans and Welk liked Bobby so much, he stayed until the show ended in 1982 and has continued to appear on specials ever since. He married Kristin Floren, the daughter of *Welk* accordionist Myron Floren, in 1971. He now runs a dance studio in his hometown of Long Beach, specializing in ballroom instruction for cotillions.

Lonnie Burr: *The Mickey Mouse Club*'s resident overachiever, who joined the show in the first season at twelve years old, sped through high school by fifteen, and earned his MFA from UCLA's theater school in 1964, by age twenty. He remained in show business, appearing in films (*Sweet Charity, Newsies, Hook*), on television (*The Beverly Hillbillies, Hill Street Blues, Chicago Hope*), and on stage (*42nd Street*). He's also a published author, with works including *Two for the Show: Great 20th Century Comedy Teams* and a memoir, *Confessions of an Accidental Mouseketeer.* His ears from the twenty-fifth anniversary celebration are the ones on display in the Smithsonian's pop culture exhibit.

Tommy Cole: An impressive singer when he signed on from the beginning of *The Mickey Mouse Club* at thirteen years old, Tommy would give up crooning for a more practical career in show business—makeup artistry. He worked for ABC and NBC before going freelance in the '70s. He was nominated for Emmys for his work on TV movies *Masquerade Party* in 1975 and *Once Upon a Brothers Grimm* in 1978 before winning in 1979 for *Backstairs at the White House,* making him the only Mouseketeer to ever receive a major Hollywood award. He was nominated three more times after that, in 1988 for *Right to Die,* in 1996 for the series *Wings,* and in 2000 for the TV special *Gepetto.* He continues to work in various leadership roles in the makeup artists' union, representing the guild on the Academy of Television Arts and Sciences Board of Governors.

Tim Considine: Tim gained fame as Spin in *The Mickey Mouse Club* serial *The Adventures of Spin and Marty* at age fourteen—then went on to play Frank in *The Hardy Boys* serials and Steve in the *Annette* segment. He later achieved teen idol status as oldest brother Mike Douglas on the long-running sitcom *My Three Sons*. He left show business behind in his twenties and instead took up writing and photography, specializing in automotive and sports reporting. He has authored several books, including *The Photographic Dictionary of Soccer*, *The Language of Sport*, and *American Grand Prix Racing: A Century of Drivers and Cars*. He has written about his *Spin and Marty* costar-turned-auto-designer David Stollery for auto industry publications, and the two did a cameo appearance together in the 2000 TV movie *The New Adventures of Spin and Marty: Suspect Behavior*.

Eileen Diamond (now Rogosin): The second-season Mouseketeer won producers over with her extraordinary ballet and modern dance skills at age thirteen. After her one season on the show, she went on to appear in uncredited dance roles in several films, including *Babes in Toyland*, *The Music Man*, and *Harum Scarum*. She also worked as a casting director and local theater producer. In 1964, she married composer and conductor Roy M. Rogosin, with whom she now runs a summer arts program for children in rural Maine called CAMP (Creative Arts, Music, and Performance).

Jimmie Dodd: The beloved adult Mooseketeer—and composer of the famed "Mickey Mouse Club March"—was known for his gentle demeanor and his on-screen morality lessons called "Doddisms." He not only became the grown-up face of the series, but he also wrote many of the series' catchiest songs, including "The Merry Mouseketeers," "Today Is Tuesday," and "Here Comes the Circus." He remained an involved Mouseketeer even after the show ended in 1958, filming extra scenes for repackaged versions of the show that ran in syndication and leading several former Mouseketeers on two publicity tours through Australia. He died in 1964 at age fifty-four while shooting a new local children's show on location in Honolulu, Hawaii.

Mary Espinosa (now Mary Goff): Just ten when she came to *The Mickey Mouse Club,* Mary left by the end of the first season. She returned to public school and kept her performing limited to singing and dancing in stage productions until the late '80s, when she took on several bit parts on television shows such as *Star Trek: The Next Generation, Moonlighting, Cagney & Lacey,* and *L.A. Law.* She now practices energy healing, reflexology, massage therapy, and meditation instruction in addition to teaching self-help classes for the Landmark Wisdom Unlimited Program. She was honored in 2008 by the Disneyland Hispanic Employees Association for being the first Hispanic female child on a television series.

Annette Funicello: Though she would go on to become an icon of '50s and '60s pop culture, Annette became a Mouseketeer at twelve years old with no television or film experience. She grew to be by far the best-known Mouseketeer and began a recording career while still on *The Mickey Mouse Club*. She went on to star in a string of Disney films before joining forces with singer Frankie Avalon in a series of wildly successful *Beach Party* movies. In the '80s, she became a spokeswoman for Skippy peanut butter, and in 1987 she briefly returned to the spotlight when she and Avalon parodied their own surf movies in *Back to the Beach*. She announced in 1992 that she had been diagnosed with multiple sclerosis, and her battle with the disease has kept her largely out of the public eye since.

Darlene Gillespie: A poised fourteen-year-old when she started as a Mouseketeer in the show's first season, Darlene was known for her extraordinary singing voice and remained on the first-string Red Team for the entire three-year run. Though she began a recording career after *The Mickey Mouse Club* ended, her singles, while critically acclaimed, never became hits. After appearing as Alice in Wonderland during a series of '60s Ford commercials and playing small parts on a few television shows (*National Velvet, Dr. Kildare*), she quit Hollywood to become a nurse. She dropped out of public view until 1997, when she and her future husband, Jerry Fraschilla, were convicted of shoplifting from a department store. She was sentenced to two years in prison in 1999 in connection with a check-kiting scheme with Fraschilla.

Cheryl Holdridge: Cheryl joined *The Mickey Mouse Club* in the second season at age twelve, quickly winning a coveted spot in the

Roll Call and remaining with the show until it ended. She was best known afterward as Wally Cleaver's girlfriend, Julie, on *Leave It to Beaver*. She appeared on several other shows, including *My Three Sons*, *Bewitched*, and *The Rifleman*. She was also a fixture in the gossip pages, dating Elvis Presley and marrying Woolworth heir Lance Reventlow in a showy Hollywood ceremony in 1964. She died in January 2009 of lung cancer.

Dallas Johann: The ten-year-old was the first Mouseketeer to be hired and the first to be fired, so he appeared in no easily spottable on-screen roles. He lasted for only the first few weeks of filming, during which he cried every time the camera was on him, leaving producers little choice but to dismiss him. He was replaced by his brother, John Lee, who was a year and a half older than him. He went on to a successful dance career as an adult, however, appearing in *Viva Las Vegas* and *Mary Poppins*, among other movies. He now lives in North Carolina, where he directs local theater and works as an accountant.

John Lee Johann: Swapped in at the last minute for his camera-shy younger brother, Dallas, the twelve-year-old John Lee appeared mostly in background roles throughout the first season before being let go with several other Mouseketeers. He appeared in many off-Broadway and Broadway productions, including *The Rothschilds* and Stephen Sondheim's *Follies*. He's now retired in upstate New York from his second career as a substance-abuse counselor. He performs in local plays and poetry readings.

Cubby O'Brien: One of the youngest Mouseketeers, the drumming prodigy signed on to *The Mickey Mouse Club* at just nine. Among the best-known cast members, he remained on the elite Red Team for the show's entire run. He made a seamless transition to a lifelong performing career as soon as the series ended, playing first for *The Lawrence Welk Show*, then touring with Spike Jones, Ann-Margret, and the Carpenters, among others. He played in the Broadway orchestra for the long-running hit *The Producers* as well as in Bernadette Peters's revivals of *Gypsy* and *Annie Get Your Gun*. He's semi-retired in Oregon, but continues to tour occasionally with Peters.

Karen Pendleton: Often paired with the other young Mouseketeer, Cubby O'Brien, Karen was nine when she joined the show in its first year. She was a true amateur who had no more training beyond some dance lessons, and producers often highlighted her inexperience and mistakes so kids would find her relatable. She left show business when the show's three-year run ended, deciding against a joint contract offer with Cubby to stay on with Disney Studios. She suffered a serious injury in a 1983 car accident that left her paralyzed from the waist down. The incident inspired her to earn her bachelor's degree, followed by a master's in psychology. She has since run a battered women's shelter and become an advocate for the disabled in Fresno, California.

Paul Petersen: As a nine-year-old on *The Mickey Mouse Club* in its first days of filming, Paul found the allure of exploring Disney Studios outweighed any sense of obligation to be on stage when he was supposed to be. After a final clash with casting director Lee Travers, Paul was fired before the show even premiered. However, he'd go on to much greater fame as Jeff Stone on *The Donna Reed Show* and as a pop singer in the '60s. He then wrote a series of adventure novels and the 1977 memoir *Walt, Mickey, and Me: Confessions of the First Ex-Mouseketeer*. He now runs a child-star advocacy group called A Minor Consideration.

Jay-Jay Solari: Jay-Jay became a Mouseketeer at thirteen, in the second season, and snagged a high-profile spot in the Roll Call thanks to his outstanding tap-dancing. However, he was dismissed with several other Mouseketeers before the third season began, and he dropped out of show business after that. He became a biker-fiction writer in the '70s, writing (as J. J. Solari) regularly for the publication *Easyriders*. He published the collection *When Bikers Meet Humans* in 2007.

David Stollery: A veteran of stage and film when he took on the role of Marty in the *Mickey Mouse Club* serial *The Adventures of Spin and Marty* at fourteen, David became an instant heartthrob along with costar—and real-life buddy—Tim Considine. He also appeared as malt-shop worker Mike in the third-season *Annette* serial. He had one more small part in the 1960 Disney movie *Ten Who Dared*, then left Hollywood behind for his true passion, automotive design. He graduated from Art Center College in Pasadena, then went to work for General Motors. He later switched to Toyota, where, in 1978, he served as lead designer on the Celica. He now runs his own company, Industrial Design Research, in Orange County, California. He appeared in a cameo role with Tim in the 2000 TV movie *The New Adventures of Spin and Marty: Suspect Behavior.*

Doreen Tracey: The daughter of vaudevillians turned Hollywood dance teachers, Doreen became a Mouseketeer at twelve and remained one of the most popular of the cast throughout the three-year run. She toured American military bases in Vietnam in the late '60s and worked in promotions for rocker Frank Zappa, among other colorful jobs. She infamously posed twice for men's magazine *Gallery* in the '70s, poking fun at her Mouseketeer past by wearing very little besides her Mouse ears. Her essay about moving past her *Mickey Mouse Club* image was published in the 2001 NPR anthology *I Thought My Father Was God.* She recently retired from a longtime administrative job at Warner Bros. Records.

Roy Williams: The Disney Studios animator became an onscreen personality when Walt Disney recruited him as the second Mooseketeer. He was known by audiences for his burly build, his goofy sense of humor, and his quick drawing skills, which featured prominently in several skits. But he was also the originator of the iconic Mouseketeer ears, which were inspired by an old Mickey Mouse cartoon when the animated rodent tipped his ears, hat-style, at Minnie. He stayed with the studio until he retired in the '70s, ever loyal to longtime boss and mentor Walt. Even after his retirement, he often visited the lot or sat and sketched at Disneyland's Art Corner. He died in 1976.

Notes

Chapter 1

6 *"Any one of these children"*: Walter Ames, "Mickey Mouse Club Set for Debut Today as Hour-Long Fare," *Los Angeles Times*, October 3, 1955

6 *More than ten million children*: Neal Gabler, *Walt Disney: The Triumph of the American Imagination* (Vintage Books, 2006)

8 *even future blockbuster auteur John Hughes*: Tim Appelo, "John Huge," *Entertainment Weekly*, December 2, 1994

Chapter 2

26 *"Mom and I agreed"*: Lonnie Burr, *Confessions of an Accidental Mouseketeer* (BearManor Media, 2009)

27 *Canadian transplant*: Original Mickey Mouse Club online, www.originalmmc.com/darlene.html

27 *made the shrewd choice*: Lorraine Santoli, *The Official Mickey Mouse Club Book* (Hyperion, 1995)

27 *"I honest to God"*: Tim Hollis and Greg Ehrbar, *Mouse Tracks: The Story of Walt Disney Records* (University Press of Mississippi, 2006)

28 *"ordinary kids"*: Santoli
28 *attended a dance-school recital*: Annette Funicello with Patricia Romanowski, *A Dream Is a Wish Your Heart Makes: My Story* (Hyperion, 1995)
28 *"star quality"*: Santoli
29 *appeared during the ballet portion*: Funicello and Romanowski
31 *none of the producers was*: Jerry Bowles, *Forever Hold Your Banner High!* (Doubleday, 1976)
31 *On May 16, 1955*: Santoli

Chapter 3

33 *Roy Disney picked up the phone*: J. A. Aberdeen, *Hollywood Renegades* (Cobblestone Enterprises, 2000)
34 *While Roy headed to New York*: Neal Gabler, *Walt Disney: The Triumph of the American Imagination* (Vintage Books, 2006)
35 *"ABC was really Disney's last hope"*: Leonard Goldenson and Marvin Wolf, *Beating the Odds: The Untold Story Behind the Rise of ABC* (Scribner, 1991)
36 *"ABC needed the television show so damned bad"*: Gabler
37 *number-six* Disneyland: Nielsen Media Research, 1954–55 Season Top 20
38 *the fifteen-minute broadcast proposed on the memo*: Gabler
38 *"the potential for the highest-rated show"*: Lorraine Santoli, *The Official Mickey Mouse Club Book* (Hyperion, 1995)
38 *"turning point"*: Goldenson
39 *"absolute creative control"*: Santoli
40 *"You! You be the producer of TV"*: Keith Keller, *Mickey Mouse Club Scrapbook* (Ace Books, 1977)
41 *who had come up through the Disney ranks*: Jerry Bowles, *Forever Hold Your Banner High!* (Doubleday, 1976)
42 *he also knew Walt had to feel*: Gabler

Chapter 4

45 *"I saw* The Mickey Mouse Club"*: Lorraine Santoli, *The Official Mickey Mouse Club Book* (Hyperion, 1995)

46 *"We would discuss an idea in the morning"*: Neal Gabler, *Walt Disney* (Vintage Books, 2006)

49 *"That was the tough part"*: Frances X. Clines, "About New York: 23 Years in a Mouse Factory," *The New York Times*, January 20, 1977

50 *had to drop off Annette's two-year-old brother*: Annette Funicello with Patricia Romanowski, *A Dream Is a Wish Your Heart Makes* (Hyperion, 1995)

51 *off to the Blue Team*: Amie Hill, "The Confessions of an Ex-Mouseketeer," *Rolling Stone*, June 24, 1971

52 *"When performed by Sharon"*: Funicello and Romanowski

53 *shipping off for a few weeks*: www.originalmmc.com/corky.html

53 *asked her to record*: Tim Hollis and Greg Ehrbar, *Mouse Tracks* (University Press of Mississippi, 2006)

55 *"Too goofy!"*: Funicello and Romanowski

56 *"For God's sake"*: Hill

64 *soon left as well*: Santoli

65 *sizzled at ninety degrees*: City of Anaheim Police Department History, www.anaheim.net/article.asp?id=670

65 *backed up for two miles*: City of Anaheim Police Department History

65 *fifteen thousand-person capacity*: Gabler

65 *counterfeit invitations*: "Disneyland Opens," The History Channel, www.history.com/this-day-in-history.do?action=VideoArticle&id=6961

65 *party crashers were sneaking*: Gabler

68 *7,500 letters per month*: Keith Keller, *Mickey Mouse Club Scrapbook* (Ace Books, 1977)

68 *"Today I saw your program"*: Santoli

69 *"There's never been anything"*: Santoli

69 *more total viewers than any other*: "Pulse Top 10 Multi-Weekly Shows," *Billboard*, February 25, 1956

Chapter 5

81 *"Because I had never been a very good eater"*: Annette Funicello with Patricia Romanowski, *A Dream Is a Wish Your Heart Makes* (Hyperion, 1995)

83 *"He was real funny like that"*: Jerry Bowles, *Forever Hold Your Banner High!* (Doubleday, 1976)

85 *reflected a larger anxiety*: Neal Gabler, *Walt Disney* (Vintage Books, 2006)

86 *"For some reason"*: Frances X. Clines, "About New York," *New York Times*, January 20, 1977

87 *Doreen Tracey found herself frozen high up*: originalmmc.com/doreen.html

90 *forty-city tour*: Lorraine Santoli, *The Official Mickey Mouse Club Book* (Hyperion, 1995)

91 *on the road in New England*: Funicello and Romanowski

92 *memos detailing scheduled personal appearances*: Santoli

Chapter 6

96 *written by former National Park Ranger*: Original Mickey Mouse Club online, www.originalmmc.com/stanjones.html

102 *getting more fan mail*: *Walt Disney Treasures: The Adventures of Spin & Marty*, interview with Harry Carey Jr., Disney DVD, 2005

103 *"In my adoration of Tim"*: Annette Funicello with Patricia Romanowski, *A Dream Is a Wish Your Heart Makes* (Hyperion, 1995)

Chapter 7

116 *felt the gravity of joining the biggest kid show*: www.originalmmc.com/jayjay.html

117 *wanted nothing more than to be a Mouseketeer*: Jerry Bowles, *Forever Hold Your Banner High!* (Doubleday, 1976)

118 *melted into a puddle of awe:* www.originalmmc.com/jayjay.html

121 *remained stoic:* Amie Hill, "The Confessions of an Ex-Mouseketeer" *Rolling Stone,* June 24, 1971

121 *felt the impact:* www.originalmmc.com/jayjay.html

126 *a thirteen-year-old blond dancer:* Original Mickey Mouse Club online, www.originalmmc.com/bonnie.html

126 *a ten-year-old who auditioned in San Diego:* Original Mickey Mouse Club online, www.originalmmc.com/linda.html

126 *moved from Dallas:* Original Mickey Mouse Club online, www .originalmmc.com/lynn.html

Chapter 8

131 *"building crushes":* Amie Hill, "The Confessions of an Ex-Mouseketeer" *Rolling Stone,* June 24, 1971

134 *covered her loose-leaf binder:* Lorraine Santoli, *The Official Mickey Mouse Club Book* (Hyperion, 1995)

134 *did nothing to deter Annette:* Annette Funicello with Patricia Romanowski, *A Dream Is a Wish Your Heart Makes* (Hyperion, 1995)

136 *"try larger sweaters":* Paul Petersen, *Walt, Mickey, and Me: Confessions of the First Ex-Mouseketeer* (Dell, 1977)

136 *"silly tight T-shirts":* "Remember Little Doreen?", *Gallery,* December 1976

136 *"They wanted you to look flat-chested":* Hill

136 *"It wasn't too much fun going to the beach with Doreen":* Bowles

136 *"too tall":* Funicello and Romanowski

137 *got his first erection:* Hill

Chapter 9

141 *"My son is six years old":* Lorraine Santoli, *The Official Mickey Mouse Club Book* (Hyperion, 1995)

143 *"Annette, you must have an awful lot of relatives"*: Annette Funicello with Patricia Romanowski, *A Dream Is a Wish Your Heart Makes* (Hyperion, 1995)

147 *was originally supposed to go to Darlene*: www.originalmmc.com/darlene.html

147 *at first considered having Annette lip-sync*: Funicello and Romanowski

147 *"We've got to put this out"*: Santoli

151 *"I believe that I inferred"*: Lonnie Burr, *Confessions of an Accidental Mouseketeer* (BearManor Media, 2009)

Chapter 10

157 *"It seemed to me"*: Annette Funicello with Patricia Romanowski, *A Dream Is a Wish Your Heart Makes* (Hyperion, 1995)

157 *"The Mouse got killed"*: Goldenson and Wolf

157 *down toward the ten-million mark*: Jerry Bowles, *Forever Hold Your Banner High!* (Doubleday, 1976)

157 *"There are only a certain number"*: Neal Gabler, *Walt Disney* (Vintage Books, 2006)

158 *Walt Disney groused*: Bob Thomas, *Walt Disney: An American Original* (Disney Editions, 1976)

158 *was fast surpassing*: Goldenson and Wolf

158 *"What did they do"*: Thomas

159 *A few weeks earlier*: Funicello and Romanowski

164 *"After a while it was a part of my life that I wanted over"*: Amie Hill, "The Confessions of an Ex-Mouseketeer" *Rolling Stone*, June 24, 1971

170 *quietly filed a lawsuit*: Original Mickey Mouse Club online, www.originalmmc.com/annette.html

170 *making just $325 per week*: Bowles

Chapter 11

177 *"It's not that the Mouseketeers have become seedy and decrepit"*: Lorraine Santoli, *The Official Mickey Mouse Club Book* (Hyperion, 1995)

178 *as she changed into her skin-tight T-shirt and skirt*: Paul Auster, *I Thought My Father Was God* (Picador, 2001)

182 *"I've done a lot of things since that are better and more creative"*: Jerry Bowles, *Forever Hold Your Banner High!* (Doubleday, 1976)

183 *earned good reviews*: "Special Merit Spotlights," *Billboard*, March 7, 1960

183 *worked on a nightclub act*: Original Mickey Mouse Club online, www .originalmmc.com/darlene.html

184 *"I know your voice"*: Bowles

184 *"Who wants to admit"*: Tim Hollis and Greg Ehrbar, *Mouse Tracks* (University Press of Mississippi, 2006)

184 *"If having been a Mouseketeer is the only thing I have to be remembered for"*: Bowles

185 *filing a lawsuit*: Robert E. Tomasson, "Chronicle," *The New York Times*, April 28, 1990

185 *"a well-known artist"*: Mack Reed, "Jury Finds Grown-up Mouseketeer Guilty of Shoplifting," *Los Angeles Times*, August 21, 1997

185 *took up a fraudulent stock-buying practice*: "1950s Mouseketeer's Act Called Theft," Associated Press, August 21, 1997

186 *received a two-year sentence*: "Away from Politics," *International Herald Tribune*, March 13, 1999

203 *attended both of her weddings*: Annette Funicello with Patricia Romanowski, *A Dream Is a Wish Your Heart Makes* (Hyperion, 1995)

205 *"Mickey Mouse is my best friend"*: Suzan Bibisi, "Annette Undaunted by Illness," *Los Angeles Daily News*, September 23, 1993

Chapter 12

209 *criticized producers*: Catherine Hinman, "Mouseketeer's Collapse Shows Flaw in System," *Orlando Sentinel*, April 10, 1990

211 *"Here they are"*: Paul Petersen, *Walt, Mickey, and Me: Confessions of the First Ex-Mouseketeer* (Dell, 1977)

214 *would go on to sell 25 million albums*: www.christinaaguilera.com

214 *best-selling album ever for a teenage solo artist*: Guinness World Records, 2000

Index